In the end, all of our contrivances
have but one object: the continued
growth of human personalities and
the cultivation of the best
possible life--*Lewis Mumford*.

RETIRING IN ARIZONA

Senior Citizens Shangri La

Boye DeMente

PHOENIX BOOKS/PUBLISHERS
6505 North 43rd Place
Paradise Valley, Arizona 85253
USA

OTHER BOOKS BY THE AUTHOR

Japanese Manners & Ethics in Business

The Tourist & the Real Japan

How to Do Business in Japan--A Guide for International Businessmen

Bachelor's Japan

Oriental Secrets of Graceful Living

Bachelor's Hawaii

Once A Fool--From Tokyo to Alaska by Amphibious Jeep

The Art of Mistress-Keeping in Japan

Faces of Japan

Erotic Mexico--A Traveler's Unofficial Guide

The Japanese As Consumers (With Fred Perry)

Face-Reading for Fun & Profit

Women of the Orient

Insider's Guide to Phoenix, Scottsdale, Tempe, Mesa & Tucson

Visitor's Guide to Arizona's Indian Reservations

P's & Cues for Travelers in Japan

Reading Your Way Around Japan

Kicking the Smoking Habit

Exotic Japan--The Land, the People, the Places & Pleasures

Eros' Revenge--The 'Brave New World' of American Sex

ISBN: 0-914778-07-2

Published by Phoenix Books/Publishers, P.O. Box 32008 Phoenix, Arizona 85064 USA. Tel. (602) 952-0163.

ACKNOWLEDGEMENTS

I am particularly indebted to the following persons for their very generous help in the preparation of this book: Gwen Bedford, Francis Ervay, Donald L. De Ment, Fern Stewart, Robin DeLong and Sidney M. Rosen--B.D.

NOTE FROM THE AUTHOR

Considerable effort was made to ensure that the information in this book was correct and valid when obtained. Certain things such as telephone numbers and prices are of course subject to change. In any event, the author alone is responsible for the selection and presentation of all materials and opinions in the book, except direct quotes that are so attributed.

The following toll-free numbers of federal agencies and commissions provide access to valuable sources of information.

BASIC EDUCATION GRANTS............... 1-800-638-6700

CANCER INFORMATION CENTER............ 1-800-638-6694
Information about all aspects of cancer for the general public, cancer patients and their families. All calls confidential.

CRIME INSURANCE INFORMATION.......... 1-800-638-8780
Information and applications regarding low-cost federal commercial and residential crime insurance.

FEDERAL ELECTIONS.................... 1-800-424-9530

FEDERAL TAX INFORMATION.............. 1-800-555-1212
Operator will give you the nearest toll-free number.

HOUSING DISCRIMINATION............... 1-800-424-8590

GASOLINE & HEATING OIL PRICES........ 1-800-424-9246

COMPLAINTS ABOUT MOVING HOUSEHOLD
    GOODS............................ 1-800-424-9246

HIGHWAY SAFETY PROBLEMS, AUTO RECALLS 1-800-424-9393

NATIONAL RUNAWAY HOTLINE............. 1-800-621-4000
24-hour service

PRODUCT SAFETY, INJURIES............. 1-800-638-2666

SOLAR HEATING & COOLING INFORMATION
    CENTER........................... 1-800-523-2929

TRAVEL HOTLINE....................... 1-800-323-1608
Loding & Transportation in the U.S.

VETERANS INFORMATION................. 1-800-555-1212
Toll-free Directory Help

METRO PHOENIX EMERGENCY PHONE NUMBERS

ABUSE/NEGLECT................................ 269-1401

CRIME STOP.................................. 262-6151

CRISIS INTERVENTION........................ 258-8011
    Alcohol-related problems

DISASTER ASSISTANCE........................ 264-6107
    Fire, flood, etc.

FIRST-AID EMERGENCIES...................... 253-1191
    Life-Line PFD Paramdics

NEW LIFE HOTLINE & COUNSELING.............. 264-4600
    Suicide prevention & crisis counseling
    24-hours daily.

RAPE HOTLINE (Center Against Sexual Abuse). 257-8095

RUMOR CONTROL (Human Resources Dept.)...... 262-6996

SUICIDE PREVENTION......................... 275-3667
    Maricopa Health Services

INFORMATION CENTERS

Arizona State Legislature, Information
  & Referral............................. 255-4900
    Information on pending legislation, names
    phone numbers of committees, etc.

Maricopa County Information Office......... 262-3271
    County services & facilities

Mesa Information & Referral............... 964-6878
    Also 834-7777, ext. 228

Phoenix Public Information Office.......... 262-7176
    Information about city services, etc.

Scottsdale Public Information Office....... 994-2414

Tempe Public Information Office........... 967-2001

U.S. Federal Information Center........... 261-3313
    Information about federal services, etc.

OTHERS

Forest Facts............................... 244-9701
    Information about firewood, camping & Xmas trees

CONTENTS

I

SENIOR CITIZEN'S SHANGRI LA

II

RETIREMENT FACILITIES IN PHOENIX
AND THE VALLEY OF THE SUN

III

SPECIAL AGENCIES & SERVICES FOR RETIREES
IN THE VALLEY OF THE SUN

IV

RETIREMENT CENTERS IN
SOUTHERN ARIZONA

TUCSON

VI

FACILITIES FOR RETIRED MILITARY
PERSONNEL IN ARIZONA

VII

COST OF LIVING, TAXES & LAWS IN
ARIZONA

VIII

RECREATION & LEISURE-TIME OPPORTUNITIES
IN ARIZONA

IX

ORGANIZATIONS & PUBLICATIONS OF INTEREST
TO SENIOR CITIZENS

The New *Senior Power* Generation

Today's America is filled with the ferment of
many cultural and social revolutions--in sexual at-
titudes and roles; in our view and behavior toward
our physical environment; in our efforts to achieve
equal opportunity and justice for all, and more.
Women Power, Black Power and Gay Power are some of
the war cries of various of these revolutionary
groups that have become prominent since the 1960s.

In the early 1970s *Senior Power* was added to the
growing list of revolutionary slogans. Instead of
sounding like a rally for revolution, however, Senior Power, to me at least, comes through as a faint
appeal for understanding and help.

Unlike other groups in American society that are
automatically disinherited by accident of birth, a
majority of our Senior Citizens enjoy the rights and
privileges of the Great American Dream until they
reach a certain age. Then many of these rights and
privileges are callously and cruelly taken away from
them. Their sufferings and frustration is all the
more bitter because they *know* what they are missing.

With the exception of a small minority--between 10
and 15 percent perhaps--America's senior citizens today become the victims of a system and a mentality
that virtually ostracizes them from the mainstream
of life the instant they reach a certain age or condition of health. The resulting plight of several
million Americans is a tragedy and a national dis-
grace. They are both a "New Generation" and an "In-
visible Generation" whose faint cries of discontent
and pain are muted by barriers erected around them--
barriers of misunderstanding, indifference and even
a kind of loathing that grows out of our unwilling-
ness to come to terms with aging and death.

The phenomenon of aging in a society in which the
accent is on youth, accomplishment and independence
has brought on a new kind of problem that no segment
of our society--employers, state and federal leaders,
educators or churchmen--has yet made any substantial

effort to relieve or solve. The problem is being studied and attacked here and there, and minute progress is being made. But the ultimate solution must be an entirely new concept of aging and of the role of the elderly in society--a concept that must be reflected in our laws as well as our thinking.

It is recognized that people need the stimulus of challenging physical and creative mental activity just as much in their senior years as before. The proper role for senior citizens must be based on these continuing needs as well as on the skills, knowhow and wisdom they have accummulated over the years. At the same time, leisure to contemplate or do nothing but laze in the sun also has its meaningful and rightful place in the lives of the elderly as well as the young.

Arizona is not being presented as the *Shangri La* for all senior citizens. There is no such place. But Arizona has many attributes that take some of the discomfort and emptiness out of the lives of retired senior citizens, and add some measure of pleasure and fulfillment in turn. By all means, anyone who has never been to Arizona should come out and take a good look before deciding on retiring here. Such an uprooting and change in lifestyle should not be regarded lightly.

Boye De Mente
PHOENIX

Many of the agencies and organizations providing
services for the aged go by their acronyms. The
following list, provided by the PCOA (Pima Council
on Aging) and RAI (Retirement Achievements Inc.)
should help to keep some of them straight.

AARP......... American Assoc. of Retired People
AART......... Arizona Assoc. of Retired Teachers
ACSC......... Arizona Council for Senior Citizens
CAP.......... Community Action Program
CEO.......... Community on Economic Opportunity
COG.......... Council of Governments
DHEW......... Dept. of Health, Education & Wel-
             fare
HCDC......... Health Center Day Care
HMO.......... Health Maintenance Organization
MAA.......... Medical Aid to the Aged
MAG.......... Maricopa Association of Governments
NARFE........ Nat'l Assoc. of Retired Federal Em-
             ployees
NCOA......... National Council on Aging
NCSC......... National Council of Senior Citizens
NIH.......... National Institute of Health
NIMH......... National Institute of Mental Health
NRTA......... National Retired Teachers Assoc.
OAA.......... Older American Act
OAA Title 3... Older American Act Service Grants
OAA Title 4... Older American Act Nutrition, Re-
             search & Demonstration
OAA Title 5... Older American Act Training
OEA.......... Office of Economic Opportunity
PAC.......... Planning & Allocation Committee
PAG.......... Pima County Assoc. of Governments
PBS.......... Public Broadcasting Service
POME......... Problems Objectives Methods Evaluat-
             ion
ROA.......... Retired Officers Association
RSVP......... Retired Senior Volunteer Program
SAC.......... Service & Allocation Committee
SAGA......... Salvation Army Golden Agers
SCORE........ Service Corps of Retired Executives
SSA Title 18.. Social Security Act--Medicare
SSA Title 19.. Social Security Act--Medicaid

I

SENIOR CITIZENS' SHANGRI LA

LETTING THE SUNSHINE IN

The sun was one of man's first objects of worship --and understandably so because it conceived and nurtured virtually every organism of life on this beautiful planet. Apparently as a result of this seminal relationship with sunlight, the desire to live in the sun, to revel in its life-giving and rejuvenating rays, is a deep and abiding urge that, as in flowers and plants, is bound up in our organic and psychic being.

But of course not all areas of the earth are equally blessed with sunshine. Furthermore, our modern industrial system has done much to reduce--and in some instances eliminate altogether--the benefits and pleasures of the sun in many of our communities. Fortunately, a growing number of senior Americans have both the courage to respond to the intrinsic attraction of the sun, and the financial means to uproot themselves and chase its golden rays during their retirement years.

For more and more, this means retiring in sundrenched Arizona, where the desert climate gives the sunshine a rare quality of purity and brilliance, and where the crispness of the air and the blueness of the vaulted sky often leaves one spellbound with their hypnotic beauty.

DAYS OF SUN; TEMPERATURES; HUMIDITY & RAIN

In Arizona we do not measure sunshine--the richest

of our natural resources--in fleeting hours or days,
but in months. Each year, Central and Southern Arizona have an average of seven months of absolutely
clear skies, plus an additional three months of
partially sunny days. On a year-around basis, Phoenix
and Tucson, for example, have sunny weather 86 percent of the time. During the spring there is brilliant sunshine 90 percent of the time. During the
summer and fall, the skies are clear and bright with
sunlight 99 percent of the time.*

This same abundance of sunshine is also charact-
eristic of much of the rest of Arizona, with Yuma in
the southwest corner of the state having an even
better record--92 percent of the possible 4,400 hours
of sunshine each year! Even north-central and northeastern Arizona, mostly high plateaus and mountains,
are bathed in sunshine a good eight to nine months of
each year, and are only partially cloudy several additional weeks.

In Central and Southern Arizona, where the major
cities and retirement communities are located, the
temperatures are mild in the winter and hot in the
summer. In winter the night-time temperatures drop
into the 40s and higher 30s and occasionally dip below the freezing mark in some areas. With the appearance of the sun the next day, however, the temperatures climb rapidly into the 60s, 70s and sometimes
80s. Day-after-winter-day is thus marked by nearly
perfect outdoor weather, when it is neither too not
nor too cold.

June, July, August and September are the hottest
months in the desert and lower portions of Arizona,
with daytime temperatures averaging 102 degrees F.
and frequently going to 110 and higher in mid-summer.
As you have probably heard, however, the humidity in
Arizona is very low, particularly during the summer
months, when it generally ranges between 10 and 30

---

*By way of comparison, Miami has only 66 percent
of the possible sunshine each year; Los Angeles
has 74 percent; New York has 60 percent; Chicago has 58 percent, and Boston 59 percent.*

percent. As a result, our high desert temperatures are not as debilitating or as uncomfortable as you might imagine. In fact, 108 degrees in the dry air of Arizona is the equivalent, in terms of comfort or discomfort, of something like 80-84 degrees in St. Louis, Chicago or New York.

Annual rainfall in the most popular retirement areas of Arizona is also very low, averaging about seven inches a year in the Greater Phoenix area; about 10½ inches in Tucson/Green Valley, and only a little over three inches along the Colorado River side of the state.

This combination of an extraordinarily high percentage of possible sunshine, summertime temperatures moderated by low humidity, and the absence of freezing temperatures and bitterly cold winds and snow in winter, provides for a healthy, invigorating and attractive environment that is especially important to older persons, whether or not they are physically active.

APPEAL OF THE WIDE OPEN SPACES

Driving alone across the vast plain-lands of northern Texas some time ago, I was struck by a feeling of loneliness so poignant and soul-wrenching that the hair on the back of my neck literally stood up. The words from an old song echoed and re-echoed through my mind: "Bury me not on the lone prairie, Where the coyotes howl and the wind blows free!"

I was struck again the following day when I entered Arizona. But this time the feeling was one of extraordinary warmth and friendliness. Here, for reasons difficult to verbalize, the open spaces hold no terrors. Instead, Arizona's wide, open vistas have some sort of magnetic attraction that draws the visitor and resident alike, much as the sirens in the *Odyssey* tempted Ulysses and his companions.

Of course, there is an immense difference between the deserts of Central and Southern Arizona and the windswept plains of the Texas Panhandle. Here, even in the driest areas, there are cacti, flowers and birds; and one is never of sight of mountains--which no mat-

ter how distant on the shimmering horizon, serve as a
boundary, as a protective wall, against the fears produced by the thought of infinite space dropping off
into nowhere. The Arizona desert, for all of its harsh-
ness and potential danger to the unwary, is an intimate, living place with an inviting aura of welcome
that tantalizes the viewer.

There are also few if any really flat areas of any
size in Arizona; here again, even on our deserts. The
land slants or rolls or swells or is ribboned with
ravines and arroyos that present an uncountable variety of subtle sights that often expand abruptly into
the magnificent scenes that have resulted in so much
of the state being set aside as national parks and
monuments.

The number of scenic wonders in Arizona is, in
fact, astounding. These begin with the Grand Canyon
National Park, and go on to such one-of-a-kind sights
as the Petrified Forest, Canyon de Chelly, Saguaro
National Monument, Organ Pipe Cactus National Monument,
12 other national parks and monuments, nine state
parks, seven national forests, over 75 lakes (yes,
lakes!) dozens of rivers and streams, and hundreds of
other natural and man-made sights that delight the
soul.

This pristine beauty of the open land in Arizona is
the second of our greatest natural resoruces. Its se-
ductive effect on visitors and residents alike is almost magical. The combination of the warming, stimula-
ting sunshine with this sensual quality of the diverse
Arizona landscape is again especially attractive to
older persons--who often for the first time can take
the time to savor their surroundings and their kinship
with nature.

Another of the most fascinating aspects of modernday Arizona is that it is still very much *Indian Country*. There are over 100,000 Indian residents in Arizona, the largest number in any state. They represent 14
different tribes and live on 19 reservations (one of
which covers 19,500,000 acres and is as large as the
state of Massachusetts). Many of Arizona's Indians
still pursue a life-style that has changed very little
for several generations--living in their hogans and

and cabins, tending sheep and cattle, weaving rugs,
making pottery and other handicrafts, and performing
traditional ceremonies just as their ancestors did.*

LEGACY OF THE WILD WEST

The legacy left to Arizona by all of its earliest
residents--Indians, the Spanish, the Mexicans, the
American Mountain Men, miners and cowboys--in fact
provides another extraordinary feature that is unique
and makes a valuable contribution to the state's attractions as a choice retirement area.

Movie images aside, Arizona has had a colorful, ex-
citing--and sometimes violent--history. The territory
has been inhabited for thousands of years by numerous
Indian groups. Northern Arizona is spectacularly marked by a number of great volcanic cones that were active less than a millaneium ago. Long before the Pil-
grims set foot on American soil, the Phoenix area was
cultivated by the *Hohokam* (Those Who Have Gone) Indians, who had constructed an elaborate canal network
to irrigate their fields as early as a thousand years
ago--then inexplicably disappeared in the 15th century.

Just a few years after the fabulous Aztec Empire of
Mexico fell to Cortez in 1521, rumors swept the new
Spanish colony that somewhere in the north, in the
area that is now Arizona, were seven cities that were
literally paved with gold (the fabled "Seven Golden
Cities of Cibola"). The Spanish authorities in Mexico
City decided in 1539 to send one Marcos de Niza, a
Franciscan monk who had been with Pizarro when that
worthy sacked and destroyed the rich Inca Empire of
Peru, to investigate these stories and determine whe-
ther it would be worthwhile to send a military expedition north to plunder the seven cities.

A huge black man named Esteban, who had recently

---

*For more information about Indians in Arizona, see
Visitor's Guide to Arizona's Indian Reservations,
by Boye De Mente. Phoenix Books/Publishers, 6505 N.
43rd Place, Paradise Valley, Arizona 85253. $4.70
(includes postage and packing).*

walked from Florida to the Gulf of California, was a-
signed to go with De Niza as his scout. When the party approached what is now the southern limits of
Arizona, De Niza sent Esteban on ahead, making him the
first non-Indian of record to set foot in the state.
Esteban was instructed to send a runner carrying a
small cross back to Fray Marcos if the story of the
golden cities was false. If the stories were true, however, he was to send a cross measuring some 12 inches
in length. If Arizona proved to be richer in gold than
Mexico, the scout was to send back a "large" cross.

When he was only four days inside Arizona, Esteban
sent back a cross the size of a man. One can imagine
the enthusiasm with which the ambitious priest set out
to catch up with his scout.

No doubt because of his shiny black skin and great
size, Esteban was treated with considerable awe and
respect in the small Indian villages he passed through.
Succumbing to temptation, he began to dress himself in
more and more elaborate costumes of colorful feathers,
bells, beads and other ornaments. As he went along, he
also became more and more imperious, finally command-
eering a retinue of Indian porters to carry his gifts
and supplies, and collecting a harem of pretty Indian
girls.

Things continued to go well for Esteban until he
approached the mesa village of *Hawikuh,* believed to be
the first of the Seven Cities of Cibola. The Hawikuhs
were not impressed or cowed by Esteban and his colorful procession, and showered them with arrows instead
of gifts. Esteban was killed. The surviving members of
his safari fled, taking the news to Fray Marcos. Despite resistence from his Indian escorts, De Niza
decided to press on—but went only as far as the distant outskirts of Hawikuh, then hastened back to Mexico City where he reported that the stories of the
seven golden cities were true.

A year later, Francisco Vasquez de Coronado, with a
large troop of cavalry and an army of cattle, sheep,
goats and pigs, set out to capture and plunder the
fabled cities of gold. Coronado found no golden cities
but it was not for lacking of trying. For two years,
he and his men trekked the deserts and mountain wild-

ernesses of Arizona and adjoining lands, becoming the
first Europeans to see the mighty Grand Canyon, the
Colorado River and the Great Plains.

After Coronado had dispelled the great gold myth of
Cibola, Arizona was left primarily to the zeal of pio-
neering priests for almost 300 years. One of the most
famous of these priests was Father Eusebio Kino, who
in 24 years in the territory--from 1687 to 1711--super-
vised the building of numerous churches and missions
and established 19 cattle ranches. Another was Father
Francisco Graces, who was a great explorer and builder
in Arizona in later years.

It was not until the 1820s and 30s that the first
Americans began appearing in Arizona; after Mexico had
won its independence from Spain in 1821 and taken over
the former Spanish colony, including what is now Texas,
New Mexico, Arizona and California. These first Ameri-
can adventurers in Arizona were the famous *Mountain
Men*: Kit Carson, Bill Williams, Al Seiber, Pauline
Weaver and others of the same breed. Gradually then,
Arizona became a crossroads for travelers and traders
going to and from California.

The first American settlements in the territory
were in the south, where the civilizing influence of
Mexico was the strongest. From about 1830, Tucson,
which had been inhabited by Indians for hundreds if
not thousands of years, the site of a Spanish fort
since 1776 and administered by Mexico since 1821, also
began to attract many footloose Americans. Within a
decade, it was known far and wide as one of the wildest frontier towns in the West.

Following the Mexican-American War in 1846/47 and
the ceding of New Mexico, Arizona and California to
the United States, the American population of the Arizona territory spurted upward. As in the past, the
new arrivals on the scene gave little or no thought to
the rights or feelings of the Indians. Some of the more
war-like Indians therefore became increasingly hostile
as their rights were ignored and their way of life
forcibly changed.

With the so-called Gadsen Purchase in 1854, which
added a large strip of land to southern Arizona, Tucson

became American. By that time it was the largest and
most important settlement in the territory. During
the late 1840s and through the 1850s, the U.S. Army
established a number of forts in Arizona to protect
isolated mining communities and ranchers, as well as
wagon trains and stage coaches, from the various Indian groups which by then had begun to fight back.
As the Indian wars grew in volume, Tucson became even
more important as a supply depot.

Arizona was formally decreed a U.S. Territory by
President Abraham Lincoln in 1862, the same year
Phoenix was founded. Tucson was made the Territorial
capital. As the scope of the Indian wars subsided,
however, so did Tucson's role in the Territory. In
1879 the capital was moved to Prescott, where it was
to remain until 1899 when it settled in Phoenix.

Phoenix owes its founding to a group of men from
the mining community of Wickenburg, some 50 miles to
the northwest, who enlarged one of the ancient Hohokam
canals and began raising hay to sell to the nearby Ft.
McDowell army post. The new settlement, on the banks
of the cool, mountain-fed Salt River, grew rapidly
after the arrival of the railroad in 1887. With the
Indian wars ended and peace and safety assured, Arizona's reputation as one of the healthiest, most invigorating and attractive environments in the country
quickly came to the fore.

The imprint left on Arizona by its history is still
visible, not only in the continued presence of great
numbers of Indians and the descendants of the Spanish,
Mexican and early American settlers, but also in the
architecture, the decorative arts, the clothing, the
food; and in the patterns of entertainment and recreation favored by the state's residents--from Mari-
achi music to rodeos.

All these influences together have both a nostalgic
and bucolic effect on residents and visitors, giving
them a taste of the past that is romantic and exotic,
as well as satisfying some deep wellsprings of the
spirit.

OPTIONS IN LOCATIONS & LIFE-STYLES

Many people are surprised to learn that Arizona is

the sixth largest state in the union, and that all of
the six New England states plus Pennsylvania and Dela-
ware would fit nicely within its borders. Roughly
rectangular in shape, Arizona borders New Mexico on
the east, Utah on the north, California on the west
and Mexico on the south.

Geographically, Arizona is divided into three huge
regions: Desert, Plateaus and Highlands. The *Desert
Region,* which makes up 30 percent of the land area, is
mostly found in the central and southern portions of
the state. It is characterized by broad plains, wide
basins and valleys that are broken up by numerous hills,
mountains and ridges that rise up abruptly from the
desert floor. The soil of Arizona's desert areas is
extremely fertile, supporting great forests of cacti,
palo verde trees and other flora, along with agricultural products and citrus groves. The elevation of the
Desert Region goes from about 138 feet above sea level
at Yuma to 2,000 feet in the vicinity of Tucson and
both north and west of Phoenix.

The *Plateau Regions* of Arizona, from 2,000 to 4,500
feet in altitude, are the largest, making up 53 percent of the land area. These are mostly found in the
northeast and southeast and in the central part of the
state just north of the desert. The plateaus, made up
of wide valleys, rolling hills and low mountains, are
often cattle country.

The *Highlands* of Arizona, in the north and northeast, range from 4,500 to well over 12,000 feet in
elevation, and include most of the scenic wonders men-
tioned earlier. Much of the Highlands is covered with
forests. The world's largest stand of Ponderosa pine
is located in the Prescott area. The great Indian Reservations of the Navajo, Hopi and White Mountain
Apaches are also located in the Highlands.

THE RETIREMENT AREAS

The most popular retirement area in Arizona is the
Valley of the Sun, a name popularly applied to the huge
multi-branched basin-valley in the central portion of
the state where Phoenix, Scottsdale, Tempe, Mesa and
some 40 other communities are located. The Valley, for

practical purposes, stretches some 80 miles from east
to west, beginning more or less at Apache Jct. on the
east and ending just beyond Litchfield Park on the
west. Roughly speaking, the Valley of the Sun is bounded on the east by the ever-intriguing Superstition
Mountains, on the north by the Phoenix Mountains, on
the west by the White Tank Mountains and on the south
by the Sierra Estrella Mountains and South Mountain.

The central area of the Valley of the Sun is broken
in several places by pyramid-shaped mounds, pinnacle
peaks and the picturesque Camelback Mountain. The lower slopes of the surrounding mountains and central
rises are among the most exclusive homesites in the
state.

The broad floor of the Valley of the Sun slants
gently from east to west. Both the north and south
sides of the Valley also slant toward the center--down
to the bed of the combined Verde and Salt Rivers, now
dammed up at the northeastern edge of the Valley and
diverted into canals for city and agricultural use.

The Valley of the Sun marks the end of the central
Plateau Region of the state and the beginning of the
great Sonoran Desert which extends on southward into
Mexico for several hundred miles. The cities, towns
and farms in the Valley are green all year around, re-
flecting an image of eternal spring. But where the
watered lawns and parks and irrigated fields stop...
the desert begins.

Tucson and Green Valley, some 120 and 145 miles
southeast of the Valley of the Sun, rank next in popularity as retirement communities as far as overall
numbers are concerned. Other areas that are also
popular as retirement centers include Lake Havasu City
on the Colorado River; Prescott, in the Coronado National Forest and known as "The Mile-High City," and
Sedona at the mouth of the spectacularly beautiful Oak
Creek Canyon just south of Flagstaff. Then there are
dozens of other small towns scattered around the state
that are also gaining in stature as retirement centers.

The retiree thus has a wide selection of places to
choose from in Arizona--from the larger metropolitan
areas of Greater Phoenix and Tucson, alpine and lake

or riverfront communities, to ex-ghost towns. The range of life-styles is also just as varied, from attractive little houses with white picket fences, plush
apartments, baronial estates on the slopes of Camelback
or Phoenix Mountains, elaborate mobile home parks, to
tiny trailers and cabins in some isolated valley.

This is not to suggest that good, or even adequate,
housing is available to all retirees in Arizona. As in
many other states, Arizona is sadly lacking in good
housing for those whose income puts them near or below
the poverty level. They often have to spend more pro-
portionately for undesirable housing than the more
affluent do for very good housing.

Mobile homes and trailers therefore account for the
housing of a significant percentage of Arizona's retirees. The state is third in the nation in the number
of mobile home parks and trailer courts, with some 600
licensed locations in Maricopa County alone at this
writing and new ones being added to the total each
month. Approximately 10 percent of Arizona's permanent
population, and a much greater percentage of our retired winter visitors live in mobile homes.

Mobile home living in Arizona reflects most of the
modern trends in this style of life. Services, facilities and social fringe benefits run from the simple
basics to the ultimate in luxury. Monthly space rental
also runs the gamut from as little as $50 to $400 or
more, depending on the variety and quality of the
facilities and services. Parks built in recent years
typically have large community recreation centers,
swimming pools, shuffleboard courts and other amenities. Many have golf courses.

Mobile home parks are particularly attractive to
many senior citizens not only because of their economy
but also because of their recreational facilities and
the common interests they provide with other residents.
Also of importance is the 24-hour surveillance provided by many parks, along with a fence that surrounds
the courts, and the one common entrance/exit.

Some parks and courts accept only permanent residents. Others will take trailers on a daily, weekly,
monthly and seasonal basis. More and more of the mobile home subdivisions are selling spaces instead of

renting or leasing them.

In Arizona, mobile homes that are 8'x40' and over
(or 12'x36') are assessed as unsecured personal property for tax purposes. Travel trailers and mobile
homes are registered as vehicles, and must have annual licenses. The manufacturer's list price is used
as the beginning value of the mobile home. The a-
sessment value is then reduced each year for a period
of 15 years, after which it is assessed at the same
value for the remainder of its use.

There are well over 200 licensed mobile home dealers in Arizona, and several mobile home manufacturers
--including the largest maker in the country. The
most popular dimensions in mobile homes are 12 x 60
feet. Some of them measure 24 x 60 or 70 feet when
expanded.

A word of caution. Mobile home living in mobile
home parks or licensed areas is quite different from
living in conventional private homes and apartments.
Those who are interested in this style of living are
advised to learn as much as possible about these dif-
ferences before committing themselves. The best way
to go about this is to talk to residents of mobile
home parks until you are satisfied that you have a
balanced perspective of both the advantages and disadvantages.

It is also very important that you thoroughly investigate any mobile home park before moving into it.
The requirements, services and general atmosphere
differ widely in individual parks. The latter, especially, can usually be determined only by talking
casually and at length with several residents.*

THE WELCOME MAT IS OUT

Arizona has still another attraction that, for
lack of a better phrase, is like icing on cake. This

*Many of the trailer and mobile home parks in Arizona
are members of the Arizona Mobile Home Association.
For a directory of members, and current rates for
the majority, write the Association at 3014 N. 53rd
Pl., Phoenix, Arizona 85018. Tel 959-1780. Send $2.

added attraction is the friendliness and hospitality
of the people...whether they have been residents for a
life-time or just a few months. The overt friendliness
of Arizonans obviously has something to do with both
the climate and the vast open spaces of the Southwest,
because it first becomes noticeable shortly after one
reaches the Great Plains of Kansas, Oklahoma and Texas.
Many cross-country travelers have commented on this
extraordinary change, which is so abrupt and conspicuous that it is very much like crossing an international border into a new country.

Besides the calming influence of the climate and
panoramic horizons that uplift one's spirit, it seems
to me that the immensity and grandeur of the environment has a humbling effect on people, making them less
self-centered, less antagonistic toward others; and
more prone to extend goodwill and share the human
pleasures. At any rate, even hardened, cynical East-
erners are transformed, virtually overnight, by moving
to Arizona.

Because of this attitude of goodwill and brother-
hood, Arizonans typically take great pleasure in wel-
coming friends and newcomers to share in the good life.

THOSE WONDERFUL "SNOW-BIRDS"

Most Arizonans especially go out of their way to
welcome the influx of *Snow-Birds* who are, of course,
winter visitors who come here by the thousands, beginning around November, to escape the snow and other
manifestations of cold weather in their own home
communities or summering places.

The majority of these winter visitors are retired.
They come in planes, cars, campers and trailers. They
settle in the Valley of the Sun, in Tucson, in Yuma
and in dozens of other communities throughout the
central and southern portions of the state--in plush
resort inns, in apartments, motels, private homes and
in trailer parks.

A significant percentage of the people who make
their permanent retirement home in Arizona first came
here as winter visitors.

HOW HEALTHY IS ARIZONA?

Arizona has a well-deserved reputation of being a health mecca. There are dozens of thousands of people who have moved to the state for a variety of ailments, and experienced dramatic improvements in their health. There have been many, in fact, who were told that they had only a few years left, only to recover completely after a move to Arizona and live to ripe old ages.

At the same time, Arizona is not of course the complete cure for all ailments, and the dry air and climate may aggravate some, Certain respiratory ailments become worse when the relative humidity drops below 10 percent--a very common occurrence in the central, southern and western regions of the state. People with certain skin ailments or sun allergies may also be compounding their problems by a move to Arizona.

On the other hand, medical science has shown in recent years that frequent, drastic changes in the weather have a direct relationship with the onset and seriousness of many physical and mental complaints. The weather in Arizona undergoes fewer erratic changes than in most other major areas of the country, Most of us don't need the support of scientific evidence to know that we tend to feel better physically and have a much better outlook on life on bright sunny days. This is where Arizona shines. You can count on the weather in Arizona being somewhere between good and wonderful over 90 percent of the time.

If you are suffering from some ailment and are thinking about retiring in Arizona, The wise thing to do is to ask you physician if a dry, cool-to-hot climate would be likely to have an adverse effect on your condition. If he doesn't know, the odds are in your favor that Arizona weather will help rather harm you.

ARIZONA HOME/RENT/ZONE LAWS

HOMESTEADING YOUR HOME

To protect their homes from forced sale by creditors (up to a maximum of $20,000), Arizona residents who own their home may file a Declaration of Homestead with the County Recorder's Office, for a fee of $3. This can be a very valuable form of insurance in the event you suffer sudden and serious financial reverses.

ARIZONA RENT LAW

Under Arizona's Residential Landlord and Tenant Act, property owners must notify their tenants of rent increases, in writing, before the increases take effect. On a weekly rental basis, landlords must give 10 days advance notice. On a monthly basis, a 30-day notice must be given. Rents cannot be increased during the term of a lease, but they can be raised when the lease expires. Or the landlord may request that the tenant move without notice.

If not renewed, some leases automatically change to a monthly tenancy when they expire. If you need help in interpreting any kind of rent or lease agreement, call the Consumer Affairs Division of the Attorney General's Office.

SENIOR CITIZEN ZONES

Arizona is one of the few states in the nation with legislation authorizing the establishment of senior citizen zoning districts. Retirement communities with this zoning may prohibit anyone under 50 from living there.

LIFE-CARE PROTECTION

Arizona law requires that endowments for new life-care retirement centers be deposited in escrow until occupancy, and that a reserve fund of liquid assets equal to one year of operation costs also be maintained in escrow.

II

RETIREMENT FACILITIES IN PHOENIX & THE VALLEY OF THE SUN

Arizona's largest city and capital of the state, *Phoenix* is also the leading retirement center in terms of overall numbers. The city occupies the central portion of the Valley of the Sun, and is flanked on the east and southeast by Scottsdale, Tempe, Chandler, Mesa and Apache Junction; and on the west by Glendale, Peoria, Sun City, Sun City West, Litchfield Park, Avondale, Buckeye and a number of other small communities. To the northeast is Paradise Valley, and a little further on, in the foothills of the rising northlands, is Cave Creek and Carefree—the latter one of the world's most unusual planned residential districts.

In the immediate Phoenix area, the Valley of the Sun is about 20 miles wide. Mountains are visible in all directions except for a narrow gap in the southwest and a similar opening to the southeast. Camelback Mountain, which partially separates Phoenix from Scottsdale and Paradise Valley, is a constant, picturesque landmark in the northeastern part of the city.

The official altitude of Phoenix is 1,086 feet, but large areas in the north, northeast and south are on gradually rising terrain. Many homes on the slopes of Camelback Mountain in the northeast, Phoenix Mountains to the north and South Mountain to the south are high enough to have beautiful panoramic views of the rest of the city and the Valley.

THE CLIMATE

There have never been more than 17 days in a year when the minimum winter temperatures in Phoenix fell to or below freezing. The average is 15 days a year—

and all of these occasions occur in the early morning hours between 2 and 6 a.m. when most people are in bed.

The mild winter season is usually underway by the end of November, and lasts through mid-March. Officially, temperatures on most winter days range in the 60s, but it usually feels much warmer because the humidity is low, there are generally no chilling winds and when you are out in the open the rays of the sun add 5 to 10 degrees to the temperature you actually feel.

By 10:30 a.m. on most winter days it is shirt-sleeve weather. On other days a light jacket or sweater is enough. With sundown, the winter-time temperatures drop rapidly into the 50s, 40s and sometimes into the 30s, making light top coats or warm jackets necessary for comfort if you are going to be outside for long.

From mid-March through May the weather in the Valley of the Sun is nearly perfect. Warm clear days and cool nights follow each other with comforting regularity. Occasionally during the early spring there will be a cool snap—or a hot spell, with daytime temperatures rising into the 90s.

Summer arrives in Phoenix in late May. By early June we start having 100 degree days...and higher. During July, August and early September, the afternoon temperatures are usually in the 104 to 108 range, and sometimes go as high as 112 or 113. At night these high summer temperatures drop into the 90s or 80s. But again "It's not the heat; it's the humidity!" While temperatures this high will of course heat outside surfaces, particularly metal, to where they will burn unprotected flesh, the dry air keeps the discomfort factor surprisingly low. One thing to beware of, however, is getting caught in the desert without drinking water. With very high temperatures and low humidity, the body dehydrates rapidly, and can bring on tragedy in just a few hours (See a special section on Surviving in the Desert in the back of this book).

Another important consideration: arriving in Phoenix "cold" on a mid-summer day can be shocking. To

some, the heat from the desert sun feels like they
have stepped into a blast furnace. Best idea is to
make your move in the fall or winter.

Autumn in the Valley of the Sun, from October
through November, is a repeat of the best months of
spring--bright, warm days and cool star-lit nights.
Phoenix is subjected to very few strong winds because
of the protective barrier of mountains ringing the
Valley. Light-to-strong windstorms, sometimes with
swirling dust, occur in the area four or five times a
year, lasting anywhere from a few minutes to an hour
or so each time. During the warm and hot seasons, the
Valley is usually blessed with cooling breezes. Still,
many Arizonans who live in Greater Phoenix and other
desert communities, particularly retirees, take advantage of the nearby plateaus and highlands to spend
several summer days or weeks (or months!) in the cool
alpine climate of the northern part of the state.

Rainfall in Phoenix averages about seven inches a
year. Other communities in the Valley receive from
five to nine inches of preciptation annually. Most of
this rain usually falls in mid-summer and in early
winter. While it may shower for a few minutes or few
hours almost any month of the year there are regularly
three to four months each year when it doesn't rain at
all. Rainfall is so rare in the Phoenix area that even
adults will flock to windows and patios to enjoy the
sight and smell when it does come.

HOUSING FACILITIES FOR RETIREES IN PHOENIX

Within the area bounded on the south by Southern
Avenue, on the east by 48th Street, on the southwest
by 34th and 43rd Avenues and on the northwest by 19th
Avenue on northward to the city limits, the percentage
of retired households in Phoenix goes up to 25 percent
in many districts.

In this large group are people who lived in Phoenix
many years before they retired, as well as those who
moved to the city for retirement. The majority of this
group live in private, individual units or apartments,
but a growing number are living in adult and retire-

ment apartment complexes and hotels, and retirement or adult mobile home centers and trailer courts.

The quality and cost of housing in this central Phoenix area ranges from very low, particularly in the districts south of McDowell Road, to high and expensive in the north and northeast. Newcomers interested in retirement in this large and most attractive area go to the usual sources for housing leads: their friends, real estate agents and the Classified Ad sections of *The Arizona Republic* and *Phoenix Gazette* newspapers.

Another excellent source of information about houses in the metropolitan Phoenix area is the publication *Buying Your Arizona Home,* published by Phoenix Publishing Co., 4709 N. 12th Street, Phoenix, Az. 85014. It sells for 50¢ and is available at groceries throughout the area or diectly from the publisher.

RETIREMENT HOME COMMUNITIES

THE BEATITUDES

Located at 1616 W. Glendale Ave., Phoenix, Arizona 85021, The Beatitudes Retirement Center is a complete care community sponsored by the Church of the Beatitudes of Phoenix and by an agency of the United Church of Christ, the Retirement Housing Foundation. The community is comprised of 273 unfurnished apartments in two five-story buildings, 64 garden apartments, and over 400 other units--in a 25-acre complex.

The Beatitudes' facilities are divided into several sections: *Beatitudes South,* which consists of 140 studio, one-bedroom and two-bedroom apartments in a five-story building; *Beatitudes North,* made up of 133 one-and-two bedroom apartments in a similar building; and the *Beatitudes Garden Apartments,* consisting of 64 two-bedroom apartments made up of 16 single-story 4-plexes.

A third five-story building is call the *Beatitudes Lodge,* and offers inn-living and sheltered care. Inn-living entails private living quarters with all meals taken in a central dining room. Under the sheltered care plan, residents have a private or semi-private furnished room with bath. A four-story *Beatitudes Care Center* provides licensed nursing care, in rooms with three beds, two beds or private.

Regular apartment facilities at the Beatitudes include kitchens with electric stoves, refrigerators and disposals. Central heating and refrigerated air-conditioning is individually controlled in each apartment. Each floor in the highrise apartment buildings has its own lounge for residents and guests. Each building has its own laundry room. Maid service can be obtained through the office at hourly rates. A beautician, podiatrist and therapist are available at regular fees.

An excellent dining room is open to all residents (and their guests) on either a regular or occasional basis for any of the daily meals, except the evening meal on Sundays when it is closed.

Recreational facilities at the Beatitudes include a heated swimming pool, a separate hydrotherapy pool, shuffleboard courts, arts and craft rooms, a men's club room with a pool table and TV, and a library.

Besides these and other facilities, the Beatitudes maintains a full-time social program director, and there is a permanent Social Committee made up of interested residents. Bi-weekly card parties, daily and weekly coffee parties, movies, Sunday night vespers, group bus trips, etc., are regular social events. The Beatitudes Auxiliary offers leadership in arts and crafts, provides hostesses for social activities, operates a gift shop on the premises, and provides transportation for individuals who do not drive. City buses pass in front of the community, and the center maintains a limousine which is available for groups going shopping or making short trips.

Nursing service is available at the Beatitudes on an emergency basis or to give injections or drugs upon doctor's orders. Each apartment is connected by intercom to the nursing station for 24-hour protection. Nursing care rates include the room, meals and regular nursing care. Each resident of the Care Center must have his or her own doctor. Rates do not include doctors' visits, drugs, medical supplies, therapy, rental of equipment or other special services. The

facilities and services of the Beatitudes Care Center
are available to non-residents, but residents have
priority on all existing vacancies.

The Beatitudes is open to all races and creeds on
a non-sectarian, first-come, first-served basis.
There is usually a large backlog of applicants, with
some having to wait for as long as 3-5 years if they
want one of the more popular apartments. For additional information and details about rental and other
costs, contact the Administrator at the address given
above.

ORANGEWOOD RETIREMENT APARTMENTS

At 7550 N. 16th Street, Phoenix, Arizona 85020,
Orangewood Retirement Estates are operated by American Baptist Estates Inc., a non-profit, church-affili-
ated corporation. But residency is not limited to members of any particular religious denomination. The
community is made up of 218 single-story residential
units in an attractive 20-acre desert setting in northeast Phoenix. Residency in the community is based on
life-lease occupancy, covered by the entrance fee;
plus a monthly service charge. There are no short-term
rentals.

Orangewood has five types of accommodations. The
smallest and most economical are studios for single occupancy, which consist of living room/bed alcove, private bathroom, private patio and storage space. Drapes
and carpets are furnished. There is a lounge and a kitchen for each 11 studio units.

There are four different apartment categories. First
are those for single occupancy consisting of living
room, dining space, kitchenette, bedroom, bathroom and
patio, with a total of 430 square feet of living space.
Drapes, carpeting, stove and refrigerator are furnished.

The first category of apartments designed for two-
person occupancy have a living room, dining space, kitchenette, bedroom, bathroom and patio, with the same
facilities as the above but with 470 square feet of
living space. The next two sizes have two bedrooms with

605 square feet and 945 square feet of living space respectively.

All residential units at Orangewood are provided with individually controlled heating and refrigerated air-conditioning. Covered carports are available for a small rental charge. Each accommodation has private storage space in or adjoining, and there are conveniently located coin-operated laundry facilities. Morning and evening meals at Orangewood Retirement Estates are available in an attractive dining room, either on an individual meal reservation system or on a monthly basis.

Other facilities at Orangewood include a chapel, a library, a game room, community center and a health center. The health facility is staffed by registered nurses 24-hours a day, and is connected by intercom to each apartment. A doctor is on call at all times. The health center is certified by the Department of Health, Education and Welfare as a participating facility under Medicare.

The monthly service charge at Orangewood (paid in addition to the life-time lease fee) covers full use of the facilities and recreation areas, basic linen service, heavy housekeeping, maintenance, utilities, the daily noon meal, off-street parking, and medical care according to an agreement supplementing Medicare benefits on a life-time basis.

There is usually a waiting list of people wanting to get into Orangewood. For some apartments, especially the larger two-bed room units, the wait may be two years or more. Anyone wishing to be put on the waiting list must make a $200 non-refundable deposit. For a couple the deposit is $300. A physical examination by an Orangewood physician is required at the time of entrance. The cost of this examination is covered by the deposit.

For other information, current lease fees, monthly service charges and availability of accommodations, contact American Baptist Estates, Inc., 7550 N. 16th St., Phoenix, Arizona 85020.

DESERT CREST

Also in northeast Phoenix near the base of Squaw
Peak (in the Phoenix Mountains), *Desert Crest* is one
of the seven retirement facilities operated by Pacific
Homes, a non-profit corporation of The United Methodist Church, and is open to all faiths and races.

One of the first of the senior citizen communities
in Arizona, this attractive center includes 124 individual residential units in a natural desert setting
of 18 acres at 2101 E. Maryland Ave., Phoenix, Arizona
85016. Accommodations include single apartments, semi-
suites, two-bedroom apartments, and both one-and-two
bedroom cottages.

One-story construction is the mode throughout Desert Crest. The grounds are landscaped to enhance the
native cacti, trees and shrubs of the desert environment. Covered walkways join all of the accommodations,
the community rooms and the dining room.

Desert Crest's apartments for single occupancy have
a large living room/bedroom combination, a kitchenette
and a bathroom, with total floor space of over 700
square feet. The semi-suites have a living room, bed
alcove, kitchenette and bathroom—for single or double
occupancy.

The two-room apartments have a full separate bedroom. All of the apartments have large porches. The
one-bedroom cottages have a full kitchen, a utility
room, a storage room, front and rear patios and a
carport. The two-bedroom apartments have two baths,
two storage rooms and three patios; thus providing separate facilities for two occupants.

Residence at Desert Crest is on a life-lease basis,
and is limited to persons who are ambulatory, in good
health for their years, and able to care for themselves without supervision or assistance at the time of
entrance. The cost of the life-time lease is called an
Accommodation Fee, and is a cash payment. The monthly
service charge is called a Continuing Care Fee, and
may be paid monthly or prepaid based on age and life
expectancy. There is a non-refundable entrance fee
which covers a required physical examination.

The Continuing Care Fee includes three meals a day in the dining room; bed and bath lines once a week; house-cleaning, utilities (except telephone); maintenance and yard work; security guard; medical care and nursing care. Desert Crest pays all costs of medical care not covered by Part A and Part B of Medicare, except for pre-existing conditions. There is also a Limited Continuing Care Plan, which includes all the services listed above, except that the only medical care provided is general nursing care, without limit, in a Corporation medical facility.

Another plan also available at Desert Crest is an Early Retirement Program, for those who want to retire at a minimum age of 55. Under this plan, residents may participate in all services except medical care, but may use up to 12 days per calendar year in the center nursing unit.

Medical facilities at Desert Crest include a 66-bed convalescent hospital with licensed nurses on duty at all times, several visiting staff doctors, and its own pharmacy.

Recreational facilities at Desert Crest include a workshop, a complete ceramic room, lapidary room, flower arranging materials, a heated swimming pool and shuffleboard courts. Among the social and cultural activities at the retirement community: square dancing, sewing bees, book review sessions, recorded concert programs and outings.

Special Note: Desert Crest has been undergoing financial reorganization, and the various programs and plans described above may have changed. Contact directly for current details. Tel 264-6427.

RETIREMENT APARTMENTS & HOTELS

CAMLU (PHOENIX)

The Phoenix member of the rapidly growing Camlu Apartment chain (there are other centers in Mesa, Tucson, etc.), is at 2935 N. 18th Pl., Phoenix, Arizona 85016, near Doctor's Hospital and a shopping center.

Designed and operated for the actively retired,

Camlu offers its residents three full meals daily--
cooked on the premises and served cafeteria style; and
once-a-week maid service. There is ample security,
with intercoms in all apartments, and a resident manager.

Other facilities at Camlu include hobby and craft
rooms, a library, TV room, and complimentary van transportation to nearby shopping, doctors and banks. Residency is based on a monthly fee. Tel 265-9813.

CHALET CARE CENTER
At 2302 E. Thomas Rd., Phoenix, Az. 85016, the Chalet Care Center is a licensed supervisory care home
for any age. Residents must be ambulatory. Tel 956-
8135.

CIRCLE PALMS
In a quiet residential neighborhood near the downtown area (2521 N. 3rd St., Phoenix, Az. 85004), Circle Palms is a senior resident apartment complex for
men and women who are 62 and older. Private and semi-
private apartments, air-conditioned and all on the
ground floor, rent by the month.

Three meals are served daily in the main dining
room, and there is weekly maid service. Recreational
and social activities are available. There is a game
room and a library. Tel 258-4614.

COUNTRY MANOR GUEST HOME
Designed to have a home-like atmosphere, the Country Manor Guest Home, 2815 N. 48th St., Phoenix, Az.
85008, provides all services for short-term and long-
term ambulatory residents. This includes meals, maid
service, laundry, beauty care, recreational activities
and shopping. Tel 959-3940.

FELLOWSHIP MANOR
A church-operated family style retirement home,
Fellowship Manor is billed as a home-away-from-home
for the healthy adult. Meals are served family style.
The attractive home is located on an acre-plus of

landscaped grounds. The Manor is at 3509 McDowell Rd.,
Phoenix, Az. 85008. Tel 267-8761.

FELLOWSHIP TOWERS
   This is a 17-story building with 180 apartments, at
222 E. Indianola Ave., Phoenix, Az. 85012. The facility is sponsored by the Arizona Odd Fellows & Rebekahs,
and operated by Arizona Odd Fellow/Rebekah Housing,
Inc., a non-profit organization.
   Apartments in Fellowship Towers include efficienci-
es, which rent for the lowest amount; small bedroom
apartments that are the next step up in price, and
large bedroom apartments--all very reasonably priced.
   To be eligible for residency in Fellowship Towers,
an applicant must be 62 or older if single; ambulatory,
in reasonably good health and able to provide self-
care. In the case of a couple, one of the applicants
may be under the age of 62. There is also a limit on
income.
   All the apartments are furnished with carpeting,
drapes, electric ranges, refrigerators and garbage disposals, and have two clothes closets, a linen closet
and a storage room. All also have invididually controlled heating and air-conditioning, safety locks and
a door intercom system.
   There is a large recreation room, a hobby room and
a coffee bar on the ground floor of Fellowship Towers.
The 17th floor is devoted entirely to community use,
and includes a large lounge with fireplace, a billiards room, TV center, coin-operated utility room,
sewing and art center, coffee bar, conference room,
card room, a promenade deck and four covered patios.
The area around the Towers is attractively landscaped
and has a patio, shuffleboard courts and parking area.
It is located in the central area of Phoenix in a
prestige district.
   Inquiries and applications for apartments should be
sent to: Admissions Committee, Arizona Odd Fellow/Re-
bekah Housing Inc., at the above address. There is a
waiting list, and a deposit equal to one month's rent
is required at the time an application is accepted.
Tel 266-9438.

PHOENIX MANOR

A rental apartment community for retired and semi-retired persons who are 50 and older, Phoenix Manor is owned by the Boswell Shaw Construction Co. of California, which owns similar communities in Sacramento, San Diego and other cities.

The 20-acre complex is divided into two sections: Phoenix Manor Number One, and Number Two. The first section contains small apartments; the second one has larger, more elaborate apartments. Altogether there are 450 units, with complete kitchens included. The complex consists of two 2-story buildings and several single-story structures. All of the apartments are single-level.

Recreational and social facilities at Phoenix Manor include two large club houses that contain rooms for card-playing, dancing, dinners, meetings, hobbies, games and TV-watching. There is also a community library. Outside facilities range from six separate shuffleboard courts, croquet, horseshoe pits, a putting green, two large swimming pools, to a heated 10-jet Jacuzzi hydrotherapy pool. Use of these facilities is free to residents. For aesthetic purposes, there are three pavilions with decorative ponds and lighted fountains.

Phoenix Manor welcomes walk-in visitors, and will show available apartments any weekday from 10 a.m. to 6 p.m., excluding the noon hour.

Rents at Phoenix Manor are FHA approved and controlled, and include all utilities, wall-to-wall carpeting, blinds and drapes, heating and refrigerated air-conditioning. Carports and community laundries are also available. Phoenix Manor is located at 2636 N. 41st Ave., Phoenix, Az 85009. Rental office telephone is 272-0496.

KIVEL MANOR

A large triple-building apartment complex designed to provide excellent housing and a program of daily activities for elderly couples, Kivel Manor is one of the most popular retirement centers in Phoenix. Applicants must be 62 or older, able to manage a small

apartment, in reasonably good health, willing to eat
one meal per day in the Manor dining room, and be in
the "upper low" to moderate income bracket.

The three highrise apartment buildings making up
the center are adjacent to Kivel Nursing Home. There
are a total of 257 apartments in the complex, including studio and one-bedroom apartments.

The waiting list at Kivel Manor is long, with some
applications pending for two years. For additional
information, contact: Administrator, Kivel Manor,
3040 N. 36th St., Phoenix, Az. 85016. Tel 956-0150.

SENIOR CITIZENS' TOWERS

Operated by the Trustees of Phoenix Memorial Hospital on a non-profit basis, the Senior Citizen's
Towers consist of two 10-story apartment buildings,
with a total of 153 apartments designed especially
for retirement living.

Tenants at Senior Citizens' Towers must be 62 or
over, except in the case of a married couple, when
one may be under 62; or if they have a physical han-
dicap. If two unmarried men or women wish to rent an
apartment together, both must be 62 or older. Residents must be able to care for their personal needs
and move about, at least with wheelchair support.

Accommodations at Senior Citizens' Towers include
studio apartments, one-bedroom apartments and two
bedroom units. All are air-conditioned. Very economical rent includes utilities, electric stove and
refrigerator, and 24-hour security service. Medical
services and other health care are available from
the adjoining hospital. Residents get special rates
on drugs from the hospital pharmacy. A particular
disadvantage of these retirement apartments is that
they are in an area where there are no nearby shopping and service facilities.

For additional information, contact the Superin-
tendant at 1401 S. 7th Ave., Phoenix, Az 85007.

PHOENIX RESIDENT HOTEL
    Operated by a division of National Accommodations,
Inc., the plush Phoenix Resident Hotel offers 43 rooms,
private or semi-private, on a daily, weekly or monthly
basis. Monthly rates are reasonably priced, and include all meals, maid and cleaning service, along with
transportation for shopping and golfing.
    The hotel boasts a well-equipped recreational cent-
er for community use. A full-time social director
plans and supervises daily activities such as sightseeing, games and parties. Facilities on the premises include a beauty salon and barber shop.
    There is no minimum age limit at the hotel, but most
permanent residents are in their 60s or older. The
hotel is at 1310 E. McDowell Rd., Phoenix, Az 85006,
adjacent to a 24-hour medical center. Tel 258-7488.

ARIZONA SENIOR CITIZEN GUEST LODGE
    This small, attractive facility has private rooms
and apartments for the elderly. Home-cooked meals are
served, and there is 24-hour service. Rates are economical. Address: 5602 N. 7th St., Phoenix, Az 85020.
Tel 248-9310.

HANCOX DESERT LODGE APARTMENTS
    Sponsored by the Desert Mission, a non-profit corp-
oration, these retirement apartments are adjacent to
the John C. Lincoln Hospital in the Sunnyslope district of north Phoenix, where the ratio of retired
households is probably the highest in the city. The
complex includes 141 apartments in a five-story building. Residents must be 62 or older.
    The apartments are managed by the Beatitudes Re-
tirement Center, 1616 W. Glendale Ave. Phoenix, Az.
85021. For more details about the Hancox Desert Lodge
contact the Administrator's Office at the Beatitudes,
tel 995-2611.

CASITA VERDE CO-OP APARTMENTS
    There are 12 two-bedroom apartments in this comp-
plex, plus a garden apartment. Grounds are spacious
and there is a swimming pool. The co-op provides low-

cost housekeeping and cooking for all the residents. There is a live-in housemother. Fees are by the month and include all groceries and heavy housekeeping. Residents have kitchen privileges and cook their own breakfasts and dinners. The noon meal is cooked and served by the housemother, who does all of the grocery shopping.

Maid service for heavy housekeeping is provided once a week. Residents are expected to take care of their day-to-day cleaning. For a brochure and other information, write Casita Verde Co-Op, 2705 E. Campbell Ave., Phoenix, Az 85016, or call 955-1896.

RETIREMENT & ADULT MOBILE HOME COMMUNITIES IN PHOENIX

There are several dozen adult and retirement trailer and mobile home parks in Phoenix. It is of course advisable for anyone interested in this style of living to visit several of the parks or courts before deciding on where to settle. The following list includes parks in Phoenix proper that cater to either adults or retires, or both.

PARADISE HO--This is a luxury adult mobile home subdivision at 14th Street and Bell Road in Paradise Valley. The fenced-in community is made up of 44 large lots (some with their own individual fences) that are meticulously landscaped to set off "fashion manor model homes."

All of the lots have been sold by the original developer, but one or more of the homes-plus-lot are regularly up for resale. Some of these resales have been handled by Leininger & Augustine, 16848 Cave Creek Rd., Paradise Valley. Tel 992-9750.

A-1 TRAILER PARK--3348 E. Washington, Phoenix, Az. 85034. Tel 275-0940. Thirty-one spaces, in an older part of town. Mature shade trees. Near city bus stop.

ARIZONA TRAILER CORRAL--902 E. Devonshire, Phoenix, Az. 85014. Tel 279-1887. Medium-sized park with recreational hall; trailers for rent.

BIG PALM MOBILE HOME PARK--1342 N. 48th St., Phoenix, Az 85008. Tel 275-0196. Huge palm trees provide shade for 34 mobile homes. Facilities include a rec hall, swimming pool, shuffleboard court. The utilities are underground.

BIG PINE MOBILE HOME PARK--1328 N. 48th St., Phoenix, Az 85008. Tel 275-2853. Mature shade trees, paved streets, city sewer hookups, natural gas. Amenities include a swimming pool, rec hall and shuffleboard court. 142 spaces.

BONAVENTURE MOBILE HOME PARK--19401 N. 7th St., (1 mile north of Bell Rd.), Phoenix, Az 85024. Tel 942-7000. A planned mobile home community, with a security wall and lighted streets, BonaVenture has city water and sewerage and underground utilities. Two-thirds of the large park is reserved for adults. Recreational facilities take up 2½ acres and include an air-conditioned rec hall, sauna bath and shuffleboard courts. Laundry and drycleaning facilities are available.

CANYON ACRES TRAILER RANCH--8208 N. Black Canyon Hiway, Phoenix, Az 85021. Tel 995-8076. Fifty-five spaces just off the freeway, and near Metro Center shopping mecca.

CATALINA MOBILE HOME PARK--1001 N. 43rd Ave., Phoenix, Az 85009. Tel 272-0830. A large park (221 spaces) with a swimming pool and rec hall.

*CASA DEL SOL 1 AND 2--Casa del Sol 1 and 2 are luxurious mobile home retirement resorts located within a short distance of each other between Phoenix and Sun City. Both are park-like in setting, with numerous trees and shrubs, and have a wide range of recreational facilities, including swimming pools, club houses, game rooms and golfing.

As a security measure the mobile home resorts each have only one entrance/exit. The streets are lighted and there are security guards on duty. Casa del Sol 1 is at 11411 N. 91st Ave., Peoria, Az 85345. Tel 797-6913. Casa del Sol 2 is at 10960 N. 67th Ave., Glendale, Az 85304. Tel 797-6988.

These two plush, resort retirement facilities belong under the Peoria and Glendale headings.

CASA DE FRANCISCO--303 S. Mountain Ave., Phoenix, Az 85040. Tel 268-7522. Affiliated with the Thunderbird Country Club, the Casa De Francisco Adult Resort Mobile Home Park has 203 spaces and its own recreational facilities. Near the base of South Mountain.

COPPER KETTLE TRAILER VILLA--16005 N. 32nd St., Phoenix, Az 85032. Tel 992-3140. In the Paradise Valley district of North Phoenix, this large park (164 spaces) has a rec hall, swimming pool and shuffleboard court.

DESERT SAGE MOBILE MANOR--1509 N. 46th St., Phoenix, Az 85008. Tel 275-1856. Popular with winter visitors as well as permanent residents. Recreational hall, swimming pool and shuffleboard.

EL DORADO MOBILE HOME PARK--4235 E. McDowell Rd., Phoenix, Az 85008. Tel 275-3033. Close to Papago Park and shopping. Swimming pool, rec hall, shuffleboard court. Underground utilities, offstreet parking, bus stop nearby.

GRANDVIEW MOBILE HOME PARK--2526 N. 32nd St., Phoenix, Az 85008. Tel 956-2140. A medium-sized park with a recreation hall and shuffleboard court.

HIGHLAND TERRACE--11801 N. 19th Ave., Phoenix, Az 85029. Tel 943-8839. Has 66 lots for 12 to 24' widths. Swimming pool, recreation hall, shuffleboard. Awnings and carports.

HI-VIEW MOBILE HOME PARK--11735 N. 19th Ave. Phoenix, Az 85029. Tel 944-8030. Trailers for rent. Near shopping center. Dusk to dawn lighting. The usual recreational facilities.

HOLIDAY SPA--10401 N. Cave Creek Rd., Phoenix, Az 85020. Tel 944-5770. A huge place with a swimming pool, hot hydrotherapy pool, recreation hall, shuffleboard and planned recreation programs.

LEISURE TIME MOBILE PARK--7000 W. Butler Dr., (off Grand Avenue at 71st Avenue), Glendale, Az 85303. Tel 931-2660. Large, modern park with separate adult and family areas. Numerous facilities.

MICHIGAN TRAILER PARK--3135 Grand Ave., Phoenix, Az 85017. Tel 269-0122. The Hayden Plaza West Shopping Center is just across the street from this large park. City sewer, water, gas, electricity, plus a variety of recreational and service facilities.

NEW HOME MOBILE PARK--2601 W. Missouri Ave., Phoenix, Az 85017. Tel 242-0098. A medium-sized park with rock and stone landscaping; no maintenance outside of trailers except for watering trees and cleaning patios. Swimming pool and recreation hall.

OREGON TRAIL MOBILE HOME PARK--8245 N. 27th Avenue, Phoenix, Az 85021. Tel 995-8080. Large park, with lots of trees. Swimming pool, rec hall and shuffleboard.

PALO VERDE MOBILE MANOR--4139 E. McDowell, Phoenix, Az 85008. Tel 275-9811. Swimming pool, recreation hall and the other usual amenities.

PARKWAY TRAILER PORTE--5130 N. 19th Ave., Phoenix, Az 85015. Tel 242-8812. Close to Chris-Town Shopping Center. Raised patios, carports, awnings; off-street parking; all lots covered in concrete. Yard work and garbage collection furnished. Swimming pool and other recreation facilities. Excellent shade.

PERI-WINKLE MOBILE HOME PARK--2728 W. Colter St., Phoenix, Az 85017. Tel 242-0511. In a quiet residential district, but within walking distance to a major shopping center. Recreational facilities.

PHOENIX WEST MOBILE HOME PARK--3150 W. Glendale Ave., Phoenix, Az 85021. Tel 973-1255. Near two large shopping centers. Usual recreational facilties.

PALM LAKES VILLAGE--16415 N. 33rd Way (off of 32nd St. ¼ mile south of Bell Road), Phoenix, Az 85032. Tel 992-6546. A beautifully landscaped 6-acre complex that includes a private lake, swimming pool, therapy pool, club house, card rooms, billiards, lounges, etc. All underground utilities; pave streets lighted from dusk to dawn. Excellent view of the lake, golf course and mountains. Lots for sale; not rent.

ROYAL PALM--2050 W. Dunlap, Phoenix, Az 85012. Tel

943-5833. Especially designed for adult living, this huge facility (nearly 500 lots) has two sections, one for trailers and one for mobile homes. Spaces include 12, 20 and 24' widths. Two recreation halls; pool and Jacuzzi bath, etc.

SAHARA MOBILE HOME PARK--4127 W. Glendale Ave., Phoenix, Az 85021. Tel 939-2531. Swimming pool, recreation hall and shuffleboard court.

SHADY RANCH TRAILER LODGE--3041 N. 44th St., Phoenix, Az 85018. Tel 959-9850. Within walking distance of Thomas Mall Shopping Center. City bus service. Rec hall and shuffleboard. Trailers for rent.

SILVER BELL TRAILER PARK--810 E. Meadowbrook, Phoenix, Az 85014. Tel 955-6112. In central Phoenix with paved streets and lots of shade.

SQUAW PEAK TERRACE--3030 E. Indian School Rd., Phoenix, Az 85016. Tel 956-0540. Swimming pool, recreation room and shuffleboard court.

SUN N SAND TRAILER RESORT--5207 N. Black Canyon Hiway, Phoenix, Az 85015. Tel 242-8209. Year-around swimming pool, recreation hall and shuffleboard. Shade.

THOMAS TRAILER COURT--1906 E. Thomas Rd., Phoenix, Az 85016. Tel 248-9648. In a quiet area near shopping, city bus stop, restaurants, medical center and hospital. Good shade. Pool and shuffleboard court.

TURF MOBILE MANOR--15601 N. 19th Ave., Phoenix, Az 85023. Tel 942-1250. About 15 minutes from downtown Phoenix (adjoins Turf Paradise Race Track), Turf Mobile Manor has adult and family sections, with a Five Star rating. Large recreation area, with numerous facilities, including a sauna and therapeutic pool. Other features are a laundry and guest parking.

VALLEY GARDEN TRAILER PARK--3441 E. Van Buren Ave., Phoenix, Az 85008. Tel 275-0960. A large park with trees, and the usual recreation facilities.

VILLA CARMEL MOBILE HOME PARK--16225 N. Cave Creek Rd., Phoenix, Az 85032. Tel 992-4571. Features sidewalks and off-street parking for two cars; spaces for

12 to 24-foot widths are available.

WAGON WHEEL MOBILE HOME RANCH--1119 N. 46th St., Phoenix, Az 85008. Tel 275-8221. Annual rates are available at this large park. Choice of recreational facilities.

WELCOME MOBILE HOME PARK--2501 W. Missouri Ave., Phoenix, Az 85017. Tel 249-9854. A 15-minute walk to Chris-Town Shopping Center. Off-street parking; planned entertainment and recreation. Large laundry room.

DEER VALLEY

MOUNTAIN SHADOWS MOBILE HOME PARK--2802 W. Foothill Dr., Deer Valley, Az 85027. Tel 942-0290. A 25-minute drive north of Phoenix via Black Canyon Highway (exit at Deer Valley Road Underpass, go west two blocks then north two blocks), this large mobile home park is several hundred feet higher than Phoenix proper and therefore several degrees cooler in the summer. Has both permanent and travel trailer spaces; several recreational facilities and special dinner parties on Thanksgiving and Christmas.

Sun City
&
Sun City West

Sun City, 15 miles northwest of Phoenix and Arizona's most famous retirement-resort community, has now been joined by a twin, *Sun City West.* Founded in 1960 by Del E. Webb of the Del E. Webb Corporation, the original Sun City grew at an astonishing pace, and within a decade was not only the largest community of its kind in the country, but was also a major city in the state of Arizona.

The secret of Sun City's success--besides its Valley of the Sun location--is that it is designed to provide a country club atmosphere and environment for every resident.

Completely self-sufficient, with all the services and facilities an ideal community would be expected to have plus some, Sun City's popularity--to my mind at least--is not so much the conveniences and services, which of course are very important, but the beauty, the aesthetics if you will, of the city.

Many cities have areas that are attractive to the eye as well as the sentiments. But there are surely few large-scale communities in the world that approach Sun City and the newer Sun City West for total beauty of all their parts.

Besides the architectural excellence of virtually all of its public and commercial buildings, the entire city has been laid out and landscaped with the care and aesthetic appreciation that goes into the creation of a traditional Japanese garden. The integration of trees, grass, stone, water and brilliant Arizona sunshine is an outstanding example of the

living environment that can be created by thoughtful
planning and dedication to a dream.

MODES OF LIVING

Sun City, which is now fully developed and doing
a steady resale business, offers its residents three
"modes" of living. Mode One consists of single-family houses with a choice of nine floor plans and
entirely different front elevations. The variety of
architectural styles—Contemporary, Ranch, Mediter-
ranean, French, Spanish and Colonial—make Sun City
streets diverse and interesting.

Mode Two is Sun City's version of a duplex home.
These come in four variations with two different
front elevations. All of them have two bedrooms and
two baths, and the largest examples have an "Arizona" room and a dining room.

Many features such as year around electric heat
pump air-conditioning, electric kitchen appliances
and a custom quality lighting fixtures and carpeting
were included in the basic price. Original options
included such luxurious items as parquet floors,
special stone veneers...and indoor swimming pools.

COMMERCIAL FACILITIES

Sun City has well over 300 businesses and services in shopping centers and at stragetic locations
around the community. These include banks, brokerage
houses, many fine restaurants, savings and loan
associations, auto repair garages, gas stations and
others. There are six major shopping centers in the
city.

RECREATIONAL FACILITIES

Certainly one of the most outstanding features of
Sun City is the number and variety of its recreational facilities. Just a partial listing is impres-
sive to say the least: Six recreational centers that
provide professionally equipped arts and crafts studios for everything from woodworking to weaving;
numerous games and social rooms; a huge air-conditioned indoor swimming pool; four community auditor-
iums for everything from dances to concerts by Sun

City's 75-piece symphony orchestra to the latest movies or plays by the Sun City Players; a 40,000 volume library; two fully automated 16-lane bowling centers that feature electronic scoring; billiard rooms; illuminated tennis courts; outdoor shuffleboard courts (two centers have air-conditioned indoor facilities for shuffleboard); eight lawn bowling greens; four miniature golf courses and an agricultural center.

Membership in Recreation Centers of Sun City Inc. includes the use of a desert picnic area with ramadas and a skeet-and-trap shooting range. The use of these facilities cost Sun City residents less than 20¢ a day per person annually.

Sun City also has seven public 18-hole golf courses which residents may use at preferential rates, and own their own golf carts, too. There are three private country clubs, each with a championship golf course. Two lakes (one private) offer boating and fishing. The Sun Bowl amphitheatre, which seats 7,500, features world-famous celebrities and entertainment. Sun City has a 4,000-seat sports stadium which regularly hosts exhibition games by professional teams.

There are also over 300 civic, social and cultural organizations residents may join if they wish.

MEDICAL FACILITIES

Sun City has a first-class hospital with a staff of 200 doctors. The Walter O. Boswell Memorial Hospital specializes in geriatric medicine and is acclaimed as one of the best such facilities in the country. In addition to the hospital there are several clinics, two nursing homes and many private doctors' offices in the retirement-resort community.

OTHER CONVENIENCES

Intra-city buses run through the community on a regular schedule, making it unnecessary for residents to drive their cars to shopping centers or recreation centers. Many people use their golf carts for transportation around Sun City. Bicycles are also very popular for transportation as well as exercise.

Sun City has many beautiful churches representing all major faiths. There are also two newspapers in Sun City--one daily and one weekly--that are oriented toward the interests and needs of the retirement community.

COST OF LIVING IN SUN CITY

Housing, of the quality and style concerned, is not any more expensive in Sun City than in many other attractive communities in the Valley of the Sun. The basic price of the multi-dwelling homes and single family homes begins in the $50,000s and goes up to $80,000 and more.

As one measure of satisfaction, the home turn-over rate in Sun City is very low--only five or six percent each year as compared to the national average of 14 percent for FHA housing. Further, almost half of the residents who do sell their homes buy new homes in Sun City or Sun City West.

WHO LIVES IN SUN CITY

Sun City residents come from all over the United States and Canada. States that have provided the highest percentage of population include California, Illinois, Michigan, New York, Minnesota, Wisconsin, Ohio, Colorado, Iowa, Missouri and Washington.

Contrary to what seems to be popular belief, not all Sun City residents are conspicuously affluent. The majority are retired school teachers, government employees, accountants, shopkeepers, newspapermen, engineers, military officers, and other typical middle-class Americans.

The standard of living in Sun City is substantially higher than the average in surrounding communities, however, and is certainly well above the average retired household throughout the country.

THE SUN CITY VACATION PLAN

As part of its program to promote Sun City, the Del E. Webb Development Company invites people to vacation in the city for two weeks for a very modest sum.

Like residency in the famous community, the vacation
plan is limited to persons who are 50 years old or older. If a couple, only one has to be 50 or more. During
winter months (Oct 16 thru May 3) two people get a one-
week introductory sampling of what life is like in Sun
City for only $200. During the summer season (June 1
thru Oct 15) the same amount pays *for two weeks*.

This sampling includes swimming, shuffleboard, tennis, lawn bowling, golf, card parties, bowling, invi-
tations to take part in special social affairs, a gui-
ded tour of many points of interest in Sun City, and a
real Western barbecue.

Couples interested in vacationing in Sun City must
get their reservations in early (a full deposit is required at the time of application) because the program
is very popular. To inquire about the program or make
application, contact the Sales Manager, Sun City, P.O.
Box 1705, Sun City, Arizona 85372. Deposits are refun-
ded in full if accommodations are not available. For
telephone inquiries call (602) 933-0173, Ext. 234.

SUN CITY WEST

Sun City West dates from January 1978 when the Del
E. Webb Development Company began building homes on a
new 13,000-acre location just a mile west of Sun City.
The Master Plan for the first 5,700 acres of the new
Sun City West is scheduled for completion in the lat-
ter part of 1980, and will have some 32,000 residents.

Features and attractions of this new Arizona retirement center include 17,000 housing units with approximately 65 percent single family dwellings and
35 percent condominiums; six 18-hole golf courses;
one main recreation center and two satellite centers;
six commercial sites designed for gas stations and
financial institutions; a central shopping area and
three additional neighborhood shopping centers; at
least 10 church sites; a complex for professional and
medical buildings; a hospital; an area for nursing
home and extended care facilities; a fire station and
cemetery.

The development of Sun City West over the next two
decades will likely eclipse its famous precedessor in

both size and amenities, according to executives of
the development company.

TELEPHONE REASSURANCE SERVICE

Sun City's Walter O. Boswell Memorial Hospital provides a free telephone reassurance service for the residents in Sun City, Sun City West and a radius of 10
miles, which includes Peoria, Litchfield Park, El Mirage and Surprise.

Users of the program phone the hospital at designated times. Failure to receive a call alerts the hospital
staff, which takes immediate action to check on the individual's welfare. To apply for the service, call
977-7211, Ext. 301.

INFORMATION & REFERRAL SERVICE

The Sun City Information & Referral Service number
is 947-4713. It is in operation on weekdays from 9 a.m.
to 4 p.m.

SUN CITY PERSONAL CARE CENTER

Camelot Manor is a licensed personal care center in
Sun City, located at 11311 N. 99th Avenue, Sun City,
Az 85351. The facility has studio and bedroom apartments, furnished and unfurnished. Two meals are served
daily and there is weekly maid service. Recreational
and social activities are planned. Tel 977-8373.

Youngtown

Youngtown, which adjoins Sun City on the west, was
established in 1954, and in 1960 became the first incorporated retirement community in the nation. The
founder of Youngtown was Benjamin Schleifer who came
to Arizona from Rochester, New York for his health in
1948, determined that he was not going to end up in
"an old folks" home.

Instead, Schleifer proposed the then novel plan of
founding a new community specifically for people of
retirement age. It was six years before he could get
enough support from others to bring his dream to real-
ity.

Schleifer chose as his site for Youngtown a strip
of raw desert on the south side of U.S. Highways 60-
70 some 16 miles northwest of the Phoenix city limits.
It was another six years later that Del E. Webb purchased a huge parcel of land adjoining Youngtown to
the east and south and began his own retirement com-
munity--Sun City.

Unlike Sun City, however, Youngtown was not a large
scale commercial venture, and while the former quickly became an international showplace, Youngtown grew
slowly, and still today is a small, quiet place not
too different from the towns that used to be so common in the midwest--except that its residents are all
retired.

The present population of Youngtown is about 2,000,
and is not expected to reach 2,500 during this decade.
In the first place, the dimensional growth of the
town is limited by holdings of the Del E. Webb Development Company, which border the town on the north,
east and south, and the Agua Fria River Wash which
adjoins Youngtown on the west.

Most of Youngtown's residential development is made
up of single family units on relatively small lots.
There are also some 20 duplexes and a number of single
story apartments. Residential dwellings occupy about
85 percent of the town's developed land. There is no
industrial development within the town, and none is
allowed by zoning ordinances. Less than two percent
of the town's population is employed. Most of these
work in the commercial shops and stores within Youngtown.

THE PRIDE OF YOUNGTOWN

Youngtown incorporates a total of 608 acres of
which some 15.5 acres are devoted to parks and recreational areas. The pride of the community is Lake Maricopa, on the west side of town. Once a huge gravel

pit, the lake is now a showplace, set off by grassy banks, and filled with fish.

Youngtown is self-sufficient and since its incorporation in 1960 has operated without the aid of a property tax. The town owns its water system, and has its own law enforcement department. Electrical power and natural gas are supplied by Arizona Public Service.

Public facilities in Youngtown include a town hall, library, police station, community club house, picnic grounds, various hobby and craft shops, and a water supply office. Medical services are provided by a modern 60-bed hospital.

The town's shopping center contains a supermarket, pharmacies, restaurants, a laundry and various home furnishings and garden supply stores. There are numerous social and service clubs active in Youngtown.

FOUNTAIN RESIDENT HOTEL

Youngtown's only hotel is a retirement/resident hotel. The large, attractive two-storied *Fountain Resident Hotel* operates under the American plan, which in this case means three full meals each day, plus snacks and refreshments in between.

Rooms at the Fountain Resident Hotel are large and well-furnished. Each has a safety-designed bathroom with sit-down tub and hand-shower, and there is a room intercom system to the office. Resident licensed nurses are available for daily health care and emergencies, and there are licensed dieticians on hand to take care of special diet needs.

Recreation facilities at the hotel include a pool, patio, library and fireplace lounge. A full-time social director plans and coordinates daily activities and evening parties. The hotel also maintains its own bus for weekly shopping and sightseeing trips. There is a beauty salon and barber shop on the premises.

The Fountain Resident Hotel is operated by National Accommodations Inc. For more information, write: Fountain Resident Hotel, 12030 113th Avenue, Youngtown, Arizona 85363.

For more information about Youngtown, contact the Youngtown Boosters Club, P.O. Box 236, Youngtown,

Arizona 85363. Or call (602) 933-8286.

ARIZONA BAPTIST RETIREMENT CENTERS
    Several years ago the Arizona Southern Baptist Sen-
ior Adult Fellowship inaugurated a program to build
and operate non-denominational retirement centers that
would provide clean, comfortable housing the elderly
in Arizona could afford.
    The Fellowship founded *Arizona Baptist Retirement
Centers Inc.,* and developed plans for centers in Youngtown, West Phoenix, East Phoenix, Tempe, Mesa, Tucson,
Payson and Prescott.
    The Hines Retirement Center, 11315 W. Peoria Ave.,
Youngtown, Az 85363, was the first center to open. The
Hines Center, on a 7½-acre landscaped tract, has efficiency apartments and individual lodges, with central
dining room and laundry facilities.
    The housing units are rented on a monthly basis, on
a one-year lease or on a life-time contract. Fees include utilities and all meals.
    For more information about the Hines Center and oth-
er centers in the on-going program, contact the Arizona Baptist Retirement Center office at the above address, or call (602) 972-2371.

    All of the additional 40-some cities and towns in
the Valley of the Sun have some retirement facilities.
The following ones are particularly noted as retirement centers:

Apache Junction

    Apache Junction, 16 miles east of Mesa where U.S.
Highways 60, 70 and 80 intersect with Arizona Highway
88 (Apache Trail), marks one of the principal dividing
lines between the desert of the Valley of the Sun and
the brooding Superstition Mountains, and the beginning
of the famous *Apache Trail* which leads to Canyon, Apache and Roosevelt Lakes on the Salt River.

Distinguished only by a gasoline station and a few odd buildings until the 1950s, Apache Junction today is one of the fastest growing areas in the state. A high percentage of the new residents are retirees, attracted by the weather of the Valley on one side, the spectacular mountain ranges on the other side, and the uncluttered, unhurried atmosphere of the area.

Among the many attractions in Apache Junction are golf courses, restaurants, a Western town where films are made (Apacheland), and its midway location between the lake and mountain country to the north and northeast and Greater Phoenix to the west.

Apache Junction has more rainfall each year than most of the rest of the Valley because of its proximity to the mountains (16.1 inches), but it still has the dry climate and the same mild winters that have made the Valley famous. Its summers on the average are cooler than those in Phoenix. The population of Apache Junction proper is measured in the few thousands, but in the area from Bush Highway on the west to King's Ranch Road on the east (in the foothills of the Superstition Mountains) the number of residents swells to nearly 75,000 during the winter months.

APACHE VILLA RETIREMENT COMMUNITY

Near the base of the Superstition Mountain range, the *Apache Villa Retirement Community* is a project of Ray Enterprise Homes of Mesa, one of the Valley's oldest builders. It is designed for retirees interested in economical living.

Located on 125 acres, the community will have 520 homes when completed. Several choice home styles are available, and there are the usual recreational facilities, including a swimming pool and therapeutic pool.

The community is close to shopping, doctors, golf courses and both river-and-lake fishing. For details contact Ray Enterprises Homes at 3200 E. Main Street, Mesa, Az 85201. Tel 832-0540.

RETIREMENT & ADULT MOBILE HOME COURTS

APACHE ACRES TRAILER PARK--10840 E. Apache Trail, Apache Junction, Az 85220. Tel 985-9641. Popular with both permanent residents and winter visitor-retirees, Apache Acres has a rec hall where card parties, bingo and pot-luck dinners are held, and movies shown. Facilities include a laundry. The park has many shade trees.

APACHE JUNCTION MOBILE HOME PARK--P.O. Box K, Apache Junction, Az 85220. Tel 982-3231. Located in the center of the town, this park features a 6-hole desert golf course in addition to the usual recreational opportunities.

BLUE STAR MOBILE HOME PARK--11050 Apache Trail, Apache Junction, Az 85220. Tel 985-9625. Social activities here include pot-luck dinners, pancake brunches, hamburger fries and movies. Numerous recreational facilities. Trailers for rent.

PACIFIC MOBILE MANOR--10220 E. Apache Trail, Apache Junction, Az 85220. Tel 986-3613. Overnight visitors are welcome here. All the usual facilities.

VALLEY PALMS MOBILE HOME PARK--10201 Apache Trail, Rt. 4 (four miles east of Bush Highway). Tel 986-4313. Palm-lined streets, nearby shopping, planned recreational programs, laundry, etc., make this a popular park.

Cave Creek

Seventeen miles north of Phoenix/Scottsdale in the foothills of the *Quien Sabe?* (Who Knows?) Mountains on the route to such picturesque places as New River Mesa, Skull Mesa and Bloody Basin, *Cave Creek* began as a mining camp back in the mid-1850s, became a stage coach station, then developed into a shopping community for cattle and sheep ranches in the area. Over 1,000 feet higher than the Valley of the Sun, Cave Creek enjoys a milder summer climate, and gets enough additional rain to support a wider variety of trees and flowers.

In the 1960s, Cave Creek began to develop as an art
and handicraft center, and to attract retired and semi-
retired residents who preferred village life over that
of the big city. Today, Cave Creek is still small, but
is an active community that prides itself on its au-
thentic Western atmosphere and appears to be on the
way to becoming a major retirement community and residential area serving the gradually filling Valley of
the Sun.

In addition to its picturesque collection of quality shops offering such things as regional crafts, an-
tique items, Indian jewelry and fashions, along with a
growing number of custom-built homes among its hills
and snug little valleys, Cave Creek also has a number
of large quality home developments that are of special
interest to the retired and semi-retired.

RANCHO MANANA

Rancho Manana was a working ranch until recent decades, when it first became a guest ranch, and then
was developed into a residential area made up of private homes and tennis villas. Adjoining the banks of
Cave Creek just south of the main Village area, the
homes and villas are shaded by tall, stately palm,
walnut, olive, citrus and pomegranate trees.

The tennis villas are available in two bedroom, 1-
bath; two bedroom, two-bath and three bedroom two-
bath models. For detailed information about Rancho
Manana write Box 1756, Cave Creek, Az 85331, or call
(602) 488-9551.

At this point, most of the retired population in
Cave Creek have had their own homes built individually
in areas of their choice. Among the realtors who are
active in the area is Metcalfe Realty, 6220 E. Cave
Creek Rd., Cave Creek. Also Slater Real Estate, Cave
Creek Rd., Cave Creek.

Carefree

If you are within the top one or one-and-a-half
percent income group in the country and seeking a

vacation or future retirement home (to add to the townhouse and country home you already have somewhere),
Arizona has a place ready-made for you.

Its called *Carefree* and its one of the most exclusive addresses in the United States. In a state renown-
ed for its scenic beauty, the Carefree area is outstanding. In an area where beautiful homes are the
rule, Carefree is in a class by itself.

Founded in 1958 by two Phoenix businessmen, Carefree is approximately 25 miles north of Scottsdale and
35 miles northeast of Phoenix, 2,500 feet up in Arizona's most spectacular foothills, adjoining Cave Creek
on the north.

At the northern base of Black Mountain, overlooking
Cave Creek Basin and covering a large area of low,
rolling hills, ridges, ravines and secluded draws,
Carefree is a resort that attracts winter visitors of
a certain breed from all over the world. It is also a
residential and retirement community for a few hundred fortunate people who have the means and imagina-
tion to take advantage of a number of very special circumstances.

In addition to beautiful homes aesthetically situated in choice sites (on such streets as Bent Barrel,
Bivouac Trail, Bloody Basin, Breathless Drive, Elbow
Bend, Mule Train Road, Never Mind Trail, No More Road,
Stage Coach Pass and Wampum Way), Carefree has a cameo
but complete shopping center, called *Spanish Village*
from its motif, a health center, a business district;
and such recreational and resort facilities as the internationally famous Carefree Inn, championship golf
courses and its own airfield.

The Tonto National Forest is just three miles north
of Carefree. Bartlett Lake, on the Verde River, is
only six miles away.

Notwithstanding its scenic beauty, exclusivity and
proximity to metropolitan Phoenix and Scottsdale, the
weather remains one of Carefree's primary attractions.
Some 1,500 feet above Phoenix and the Valley of the
Sun, Carefree has the same low humidity and approximately the same amount of sunshine. But its higher
altitude ensures that the hottest summer temperatures

will be five to 10 degrees below those in the Valley
of the Sun, and that the air will be cleaner and crisp-
er. Winter days in Carefree are almost always brilliant
with sunshine, and warm to pleasantly cool. There are
usually two or three light snows each winter that are
gone within an hour or so.

An unusual and very interesting note: the water
that makes Carefree possible comes from a huge underground lake that is fed by subterranean streams from
the high Mogollon Rim and White Mountains country to
the north and northeast. It is held in place beneath
Carefree by what hydrologists say is a great rock stra-
ta that forms a gigantic pool.

Additional information on the Carefree/Cave Creek
areas is available from the Chamber of Commerce, Ho
Hum Lane, Carefree, Az 85331. Tel (602) 488-3381.

THE BOULDERS

One of the most unusual developments in the unin-
corporated community of Carefree is a residential area
known as *The Boulders;* so-called because of the presence of huge building-sized boulders strewn about the
desert landscape and on the waists of hills.

Encompassing an area of 640 acres, with each home
on a minimum of one acre, The Boulders is a completely
master-planned community that, among other things, requires each home to take up no more than one-third of
an acre and for the remaining two-thirds to be maintained in its natural state.

Land in The Boulders is not altered to fit the
homes. The homes are designed to fit the land, following its natural contours and set in such a way that
occupants have an unobstructed view of the immediate
desert and surrounding circle of mountains. The homes,
which have approximately 2,600 square feet of floor
space and appear more like villas, are also designed
so that the inside and outside merge and complement
each other. A golf course is similarly merged in with
the community so that it also complements rather than
intrudes on the overall natural beauty of the area.

Recreational centers are strategically placed in

The Boulders so residents have only to walk a short
distance to a swimming pool, Jacuzzi whirlpool, sauna
bath, fully equipped grills, refrigerators, freezers
and other outside facilities.

All utilities in The Boulders are underground.
There is a 24-hour security guard. Roads are private
and are patrolled. Exterior home and ground maintenance service are available. For more information about
this exclusive desert oasis, contact Carefree Developers Inc., P.O. Box 708, Carefree, Az 85331. Tel (602)
488-3545.

GETTING ACQUAINTED WITH CAREFREE

The best way to get acquainted with Carefree is to
spend a few days at Carefree Inn, one of the Southwest's most attractive and interesting resorts. Situated in an especially beautiful desert area, the Inn
gives the impression that you are in a palatial private estate. Rooms are oversize, have their own set-
te, game table, refrigerator, color TV, private patio
and panoramic view. Upon arrival guests are served
cocktails at poolside or in the El Dorado Lounge.
Breakfasts can also be taken poolside if you like.

Recreation facilities at Carefree Inn include swimming, tennis on any of five laykold courts, golfing,
bicycling, horseback riding and more. For reservations
write Carefree Inn, P.O. Box 708, Carefree, Az 85331
or call (602) 488-3551.

TONTO HILLS

Seven miles north of Carefree on Seven Springs
Road, *Tonto Hills* is an exclusive residential community that in the opinion of many is in an area even more
scenic than Carefree.

At an elevation of 3,500 feet and covering approximately 600 acres, Tonto Hills is a development project
of the E. V. Graham Company, 7154 Fifth Avenue, Scottsdale, Az 85251. All lots in the community are 1½ acres
or more. All utilities are underground.

Besides its scenic location and proximity to lakes
and forests, Tonto Hills' higher altitude gives it
more of an alpine than desert climate.

Chandler

"Where the Sunshine Spends the Winter," is the motto of this attractive little city, 23 miles southeast of Phoenix and adjoining Tempe on the south. Nationally known as the home of the San Marcos Resort Hotel, *Chandler* is growing in popularity as a place of permanent residency for retirees.

Apartments and small homes are generally available in Chandler, and there are several mobile home and trailer parks in the area. The city also has several units of public housing for the elderly.

Chandler has its own recreational facilities for golfing, swimming, tennis, horseback riding, etc., along with movie theaters, a community center and library. The cultural and recreational facilities of Tempe, Mesa, Scottsdale and Phoenix are only minutes away.

MOBILE HOME PARKS

CASA DEL CAMPO—200 E. Knox Rd., Chandler, Az 85-224. Tel 963-9747. This mobile home community is for adults only. Besides the usual recreational facilities, it has a spacious clubhouse and laundry.

HACIENDA SOLANO MOBILE HOME PARK—Gilbert Road (south of Williams Field Road), Chandler, Az 85224. Tel 963-3477. Has both family and adult sections, with lots for all sizes of mobile homes, including the totally electric, in landscaped surroundings. Clubhouse, pool and shuffleboard courts, with planned activities. Laundry.

SUNSHINE VALLEY MOBILE HOME PARK—18250 S. Arizona Ave., Chandler, Az 85224. Tel 963-4455. Very large, with tennis courts in addition to the usual pool, etc. On-site new and used mobile home sales.

VALLEY MOBILE HOME ESTATES—200 E. Ivanhoe St., Chandler, Az 85224. Tel 963-4230. Rated 5-star by Woodall, this very attractive place is in a residential neighborhood. Swimming pool, shuffleboard courts and rec hall. Space for overnight travelers.

Glendale

Glendale is a thriving, mostly residential community adjoining Phoenix on the northwest, and for all practical purposes is a suburb of its larger neighbor. The quieter, more rural-like atmosphere--within minutes of the services and facilities of a large city--gives Glendale an edge as a retirement area.

The town has a retirement center and a number of adult/retirement mobile home parks. The Glendale Community Center, 7125 N. 58th Dr., Glendale, holds Senior Citizen's Day every Monday from 11:30 a.m. to 4:30 p.m. offering many recreational activities.

GLENCROFT RETIREMENT COMMUNITY

This is a retirement center located on a 36-acre tract of land northwest of the business district of Glendale. It is owned and operated by *Friendship Retirement Corporation,* a non-profit organization founded by eight churches in the Phoenix area for the purpose of planning, building and operating full-service retirement centers for senior citizens. There are no admission restrictions as to race, color, creed or country of origin.

The large community includes regular apartments and garden apartments, plus a recreation building, swimming pool and spa.

Each apartment is equipped with an emergency call system. Covered parking spaces are available. Apartments offered are efficiency, one bedroom, two bedroom and two bedrooms with 1½ baths. The apartments are air-conditioned. Patios and front entrances are covered. Drapes and carpets are furnished. An electric range, garbage disposal and family-sized refrigerator/freezer are provided. Residents provide all other furnishings.

There are an additional 120 personal care apartments in the complex. This facility provides apartment living with the privilege of taking one or more daily meals in a central dining room. There is an infirmary on the premises.

Garden apartments at Glencroft are operated on a
life-time lease basis. The personal care apartments
are rented on a monthly bsis. For information about
current costs and other details, contact the Administrator, Glencroft Retirement Community, 8611 N.
67th Avenue, Glendale, Az 85302. Tel (602) 939-6481.

ADULT/RETIREMENT MOBILE HOME PARKS

THE BETHANY GRAND--4950 W. Bethany Home Rd., Glendale, Az 85301. Tel 937-8164. An attractive park with
street lights, large spaces, off-street parking, good
shade, laundry facilities, recreation hall and swimming pool.

BLUE SKY MOBILE HOME PARK--4800 W. Ocotillo, Glendale, Az 85301. Tel 939-5425. Near a major shopping
center, with city bus service. Swimming pool.

GLENDALE CASCADE MOBILE HOME COMMUNITY--5747 West
Missouri Ave., Glendale, Az 85301. Tel 934-4070. Has
both family and adult areas, with a wide range of
recreational facilities. West Valley Mall Shopping
Center is nearby.

GRAND MISSOURI--4400 W. Missouri, Glendale, Az
85301. Tel 937-7721. Two large adjoining parks, one
for families, the other for adults only, with maximum security. Heated swimming pool, hydrotherapy
pool, shuffleboard court and recreation hall. Single
and double trailers for rent.

PALM SHADOWS--7300 N. 51st Ave., Glendale, Az
85301. Tel 934-1308. A large park with numerous recreational facilities. Popular with retirees.

Litchfield Park

Another Arizona city that is not intended to be a
retirement community but is nevertheless of special
interest to senior citizens is *Litchfield Park,* 16
miles due west of central Phoenix in an area made
famous by the plush Wigwam Resort Hotel. Designed to

have an eventual population of 75,000 who will live
in a dozen connected villages, Litchfield Park has already attracted worldwide attention because of its
original concept for modern living.

The heart of each Village is its Village Square,
which is within easy walking distance of any part of
the unit. In the square is a school, library, park,
recreation area, a market, pharmacy, post office, bank
and the other services and shops that a community
needs to sustain itself.

Facilities within the Village Square and neighboring residential areas are connected by winding pathways which are limited to pedestrians, bicycles and
electric carts. Children can walk to school and to the
park in safety, and residents can do their shopping
within minutes of where they live.

When the dozen Villages of Litchfield Park are completed, they will center around a city *Core* of department stores, shops, restaurants, hotels, highrise a-
partments, office buildings, civic, cultural and medical complexes and a college campus. Large industrial
centers, making Litchfield Park almost self-supporting,
will be within a few minutes drive from the Villages.
The city core will be less than a mile and a half from
any Village home.

The entire city plot is divided into six communities and each community is divided into two villages.
Each village is in turn made up of a cluster of four
neighborhoods. The cultural, recreational, shopping
and educational activities of each community are located where the pathway and arterial streets intersect. Each neighborhood is designed to have from
1,800 to 2,500 residents, with a typical village having from 7,500 to 10,000 residents.

Each village at Litchfield Park is being build
around a central theme. In Tierra Verde it is the 36-
hole golf course complex of the Goodyear Golf and Country Club. Another special feature of the Tierra Verde
Village is *Tierra Verde Lake,* which covers six acres
and has its own dock for sailing and row boats. The
lake is adjoined by a park and a development area of

300 patio homes, townhouses and garden apartments.

Hundreds of acres of this attractive, planned city have been committed to golf courses, lakes and park grounds that will thread through the central Core of each of the 12 villages, providing both recreation and beauty.

An unusual pattern of streets virtually eliminates traffic congestion in Litchfield Park. Collector streets are designed to serve only their own local residents, making through traffic impractical and keeping the village streets quieter and safer. Arterial roads, beautifully landscaped, serve as boundaries for the villages and provide the primary transportation network. The arterials have access to the Papago Freeway, which is part of Interstate Highway 10 that goes through Phoenix--some 15 to 20 minutes away.

Lots are available in Litchfield Park from Litchfield Park Properties, 111 W. Indian School Rd., Litchfield Park, Az 85340 (mailing address: P.O. Box 747). Tel (602) 935-3836. Information about commercial and industrial sites for personal and investment purposes is available from the same office.

Litchfield Park Properties itself does not presently build or sell houses in the area. This is done by a number of well-known Valley builders. All lots are fully improved with paved streets, curbs, sidewalks and pathways.

Rental units are also available in Litchfield Park. These include unfurnished garden apartments near the Country Club. Residents are eligible for membership in the Recreation Center of the exclusive Goodyear Golf and Country Club.

Mesa

Mesa is one of the best-planned and most attractive cities in Arizona. Founded in 1878 by Mormon pioneers, Mesa's citizens made many of the right decisions as early as 1917 when they bought their own gas, water and electric plants, and again in 1923 when they

adopted the merit system of city government. The city
fathers have continued to be as farsighted and as de-
dicated to both the beautification and livability of
their city--which is one of the few cities of any
size in the country that has no property tax.

Sixteen miles east of Phoenix and bordering Tempe
and Scottsdale on the west and Apache Junction on the
east, Mesa is spread out along both sides of U.S. Highways 60-70. About 200 feet higher in elevation than
Phoenix, at 1,241 feet, Mesa has approximately the same
rainfall, the same low humidity and the same percentage
of annual sunshine as the rest of the Valley of the
Sun.

Besides its popularity as a permanent home for retirees, Mesa's wintertime population swells each year
with retired visitors from many parts of the country.
A great deal of wintertime activity in the city is, in
fact, oriented toward winter visitors and retired permanent residents.

Among the regularly scheduled events at several different locations are bingo; cards; dancing; movies;
sports; hikes; state picnics; adult classes in such
things as music, arts and crafts; shuffleboard tour-
naments; horseshoe pitching; croquet; chess games;
plus numerous other special events.

Many of these activities take palce in Mesa's two
major parks, Rendezvous Park and Pioneer Park. Visitors and residents are invited to pick up a current calendar of events at the Mesa Chamber of Commerce, 10 W.
1st Street, Mesa. Tel 969-1307.

LEISURE WORLD

The largest and best-known retirement community in
Mesa is *Leisure World,* which competes with Sun City and
Green Valley, south of Tucson, as premiere retirement
centers. Located about 15 minutes east of downtown Mesa
toward the base of the towering Superstition Mountains
and adjacent to the Golden Hills Country Club, Leisure
World is one of the fastest growing retirement communities in the Valley.

Leisure World offers conventional housing to people

who are 45 years of age or older. Homes are two bedroom two-bath, three-bedroom two-bath, in a variety
of elevations, all following the basic Spanish arch-
itectual theme that gives the community its distinctive image.

All Leisure World homes come with fully equipped
kitchens, carpet, covered patios and health and security systems, called *Monitor Six*. This is a compu-
terized system that will alert the 24-hour Registered Nurse service on the premises, or the local authorities. Each home has an emergency switch in the
master bedroom. Should illness or adversity strike,
the resident need only to activate the switch and
response will be immediate.

All medical records of residents are kept on the
premises so the on-duty nurses can administer prescriptions or other medical service according to the
resident's own doctor's orders.

Recreational opportunities abound at Leisure
World. There are all the usual facilities: a large
swimming pool; jacuzzi pool; theater (where residents may show their own movies); a ballroom, and a
fully-equipped arts and crafts center. There is also
an 18-hole golf course, a well-kept (and regularly
used) lawn bowling green; tennis courts and a health
spa with its own natural hotsprings mineral baths.
Clubs and organizations at Leisure World range from
Gourmet Cooking to Lapidary.

Travel and transportation at Leisure World is
primarily by golf cart. Designed "on a people scale;
not an automobile scale," the community is oriented
for walking, bicycling and other forms of slower
transportation. There is limited access to the center
by non-residents. Security begins at the continously
guarded gatehouse and includes 24-hour roaming pat-
rols. Free shuttle-bus service is available for residents within the community and to key places outside of Leisure World.

High on the list of Leisure World's attractions
is its proximity to some of Arizona's most beautiful
scenic areas. Within just a few minutes drive to the
east are the legendary Superstition Mountains, which

are accessible by car and offer hiking, picniking,
horseback riding, overnight camping and prospecting.

The famous *Apache Trail* which begins in Apache
Junction just minutes from Leisure World, leads to
some of Arizona's most spectacular lake and wilderness area country, less than a hour's drive away.

Future developments at Leisure World (by Ditz-
Crane, Arizona's second largest home-builder) include a community hospital and a full-scale shopping
center. For additional information about Leisure
World, write or visit 908 S. Power Rd., Mesa, Arizona 85206. Tel (602) 832-3232.

DREAMLAND VILLA

On East University Drive in the northern outskirts
of Mesa, *Dreamland Villa* was one of the first major
retirement centers in the Mesa area. Large and attractive, the center has been fully developed for several years, and there is now a steady resale of homes,
which range from 1,005 to 1,910 square feet of living
space.

All of the homes in Dreamland Villa are located on
large lots, with desert-style landscaping and gardens.
All have covered patios and 14-foot carports.

Recreation at Dreamland Villa centers around a
large Club House that has a complete kitchen, snack
bar, television lounge, game and meeting rooms, a
concert stage, a billiards room, and arts and crafts
shop with facilities for ceramic-making, sewing,
woodworking and lapidary. Outside there is a huge
swimming pool, 12 shuffleboard courts, horseshoe pits
and a 9-hole golf course, complete with pro shop and
coffee shop.

Dreamland Villa adjoins the large Velda Rose Shopping Center, which includes a modern medical complex.
Residents of the well-known retirement community have
easy access to other nearby shopping centers and
downtown Mesa via bus (Safeway Suburban Stages) that
operates between Apache Junction and Mesa, or the
Mesa Dial-A-Ride service.

Anyone interested in buying a home in the community may contact the Dreamland Villa Resale Office,

c/o Farnsworth Realty & Construction Co., 6053 East
University Dr., Mesa, Az 85206. Tel 832-6200.

SUNLAND VILLAGE

The second retirement community to be developed
by Mesa's Farnsworth Realty & Construction Co., *Sunland Village* followed the same successful format:
an attractive location; a well-designed and landscaped site; a choice of several home styles; all the
latest conveniences at different price levels--plus
resort-like recreation facilities, including a golf
course, tennis courts, swimming pools, handicraft
shops, etc.

Sunland Village is at Broadway and Greenfield Rd.
on the eastern edge of Mesa. The sales office is at
4500 E. Diamond St., Mesa, Az 85206. Tel 832-6200.

SUNLAND VILLAGE EAST

The third retirement community developed by Farnsworth Realty & Construction Co., *Sunland Village East*
covers 914 acres (twice the size of the first village)
and will have 3,700 homes when completed.

Among the choices of home styles in Sunland Village East are single family units, duplexes, multi-
family clusters with 10 living units in each cluster,
condominiums and rental apartments.

The village boasts 36 holes of golf, tennis courts,
pools, arts and craft facilities, and more. There is
also an 800-seat auditorium and an outdoor amphitheater.

Sunland Village East is on Baseline Road just east
of Power Road on the east side of Mesa. For more information, contact the Farnsworth Realty & Construction Company Sales Office at 4500 E. Diamond St.,
Mesa, Az 85206. Tel 832-6200.

GOLDEN HILLS COUNTRY CLUB ESTATES

A semi-exclusive retirement community, with both
adult and family sections, the beautiful *Golden Hills
Country Club Estates* presently has several hundred
residents. Additional homes are being completed each
month. Situated on 500 acres of private land, Golden
Hills is seven miles east of downtown Mesa and a mile

south of the main Valley of the Sun highway.

Homes in Golden Hills are built around the long-
est 18-hole golf course in the Greater Phoenix area.
At the north end of the community is the Golden
Hills Country Club, which has a pro shop, coffee shop,
cocktail lounge and first-class restaurant. At mid-
point in the community is the *Golden Hills Adult Center,* which is headquarters for all informational and
recreational activities.

Regular functions at the adult center, planned and
coordinated by a program director, include lectures,
potluck suppers, bridge, bingo, billiards, cards,
arts and crafts, and cultural exhibits.

In addition to homes for permanent residence, Golden Hills has apartments for seasonal and shorter-
term guests. Home buyers in Golden Hills have their
choice of several floor plans and price ranges.

Supermarkets, speciality shops, drug stores and
medical facilities, as well as churches of many de-
nominations, are located within the immediate area
of Golden Hills. The Superstition Mountains recreation and wilderness areas are within half an hour of
the community, and the first of four lakes on the Salt
River is only 30 minutes away.

For more information, contact Apache Homes Inc.,
714 S. 72nd St., Mesa, Arizona 85208. Tel 832-5122.

PATTERSON TERRACE

The *Patterson Terrace Apartments* for senior citizens is a large 4-story combination apartment complex
and nursing home located at 1825 W. Emelita in Mesa,
off of Dobson Road between Southern Avenue and Broadway.

The Terrace offers its residents optional community dining and individual housekeeping service. The
complex has special emergency and convenience facilities for the elderly, and a staff on duty 24 hours a
day.

Other amenities include arts and crafts rooms, a
game room, swimming pool, barber and hair-care. Desert Samaritan Hospital, Mesa Community College, a
shopping and medical center, plus banks and churches

are within easy commuting distance of Patterson Terrace. For more information call 964-0410 or write to: The Foundation for Senior Adult Living, 1825 W. Northern Ave., Phoenix, Az 85021. The Foundation manages the apartment/nursing home complex.

VELDA ROSE ESTATES

One of the oldest and most popular of the Mesa retirment communities, *Velda Rose Estates* dates from 1963. Six miles east of the downtown area of Mesa, at 64th Street and University Drive, Velda Rose Estates is a planned adult/retirement community of well laid-out streets and attractive homes.

Homes in Velda Rose Estates come in four basic floor plans that range in size from 1,082 square feet to 1,565 square feet of floor space. The homes have electric kitchens, electric water heaters and furnaces.

There is a large Community Center, a club house and a swimming pool avilable for use by residents. For details about resale property, contact Velda Rose Estates, 301 N. 65th St., Mesa, Az 85205. Tel 832-1511.

RETIREMENT APARTMENTS

CAMLU RETIREMENT APARTMENTS--152 N. 56th Street, Mesa, Az 85205. Tel 985-0680. This apartment development is strictly for the retired. There are 78 studio and one-bedroom apartments, fully furnished with maid service and all utilities. There is a laundry, a beauty salon, recreation room and lounges with television.

Each apartment at Camlu is equipped with an emergency intercom system. Three meals a day are served. There are many planned activities, and residents are regularly taken on shopping tours.

There is usually a short waiting list for the apartments.

FARNSWORTH APARTMENTS

Built by the developers of Dreamland Villa and Sunland Villages, the *Farnsworth Apartments* are de-

signed for the retired and semi-retired who prefer to
rent; with six-month or longer leases preferred. Furnished and unfurnished apartments are avilable and
include carpets, drapes, refrigerator, range and oven.
Rents include yard care and all utilities except electricity. All the apartments are single-story construction and there are no steps or stairs to climb.

Residents of the apartments have membership in a
Recreation Center that has two swimming pools, a Jacuzzi bath, shuffleboard courts, a billiards room,
card rooms, a library, woodworking shop and other facilities. Regular events at the center include bingo,
bridge, potluck dinners and social programs.

For details contact the Farnsworth Apartments at
5854 E. Albany, Mesa, Az 85206. Tel 832-6200.

RETIREMENT & ADULT MOBILE HOME CENTERS

APACHE WELLS MOBILE CITY & COUNTRY CLUB

One of the largest (over 1500 lots) and finest a-
dult home communities in the country, *Apache Wells*
is in fact country club-living. Facilities include a
championship 18-hole golf course, an Olympic-sized
swimming pool, a huge recreation hall, art studio, craft center, cocktail lounge, restaurant, coffee shop,
shopping center, Jacuzzi therapeutic pool, game room,
shuffleboard and croquet courts and putting greens.

In addition to mobile home lots for sale or lease,
along with travel trailer spaces, Apache Wells also
offers travel trailer cabanas that include a variety
of excellent accommodations from "quickie" visits to
year-around resort style living.

Recreational and social activities at Apache Wells
include holiday and special event dinners; round and
square dancing; desert hikes and picnics; golf tour-
naments; fine arts and craft shows, etc.

Apache Wells has all paved streets, rolled curbs
and sidewalks, service from a modern sewerage disposal plant, natural well water, natural gas, and twice-
a-week trash collection. There is a monthly service
fee which covers the use of all the recreation facilities, domestic water and refuse collection.

Apache Wells is at 2211 N. 56th Street at McKellips
Road, eight miles from downtown Mesa. The zip code is
85205. Tel 832-1550.

FOUNTAIN OF THE SUN
A luxurious combination conventional housing and
mobile home community, with lot purchase only, *Fountain of the Sun* is built around an 11-acre central
park with an 18-hole golf course, lake and casting
pond.

Other recreational facilities include shuffleboard,
tennis courts, putting green, billiards, driving
range, horseshoe pits, large swimming pool, sauna and
therapy pools. A huge Community Center has a party/
ballroom and work areas for handicrafts and games.

Golf cart paths and walking trails wind around the
community. Streets are paved, all utilities are underground, and there is 24-hour gatehouse and security
guard service.

Fountain of the Sun is open to visitors from 8:30
a.m. to 7 p.m. daily. Write or call for a booklet
giving full details about this beautifully planned
retirement center. Address: 8001 E. Broadway, Mesa,
Az 85208. Tel (602) 832-2600.

MESA EAST
An elaborate adult mobile home community, *Mesa
East* is on Apache Trail (which is what U.S. Highways
60 & 70 are called between Mesa and Apache Junction),
seven miles east of Mesa. Focal point of the community is a large Recreation Center in a central 3-acre
park.

Besides all the usual recreational equipment, Mesa
East has regularly scheduled activities ranging from
yoga classes, arts and crafts and card games to potluck dinners. A major shopping center is two minutes
away. There are three large hospitals within 15 minutes. Fishing and boating lakes are within half an
hour's drive.

For details, contact Mesa East, 225 S. 74th Street,
Mesa, Az 85207. Tel (602) 985-1160.

CIELO GRANDE MOBILE HOME PARK

Cielo Grande Mobile Home Park is large and attractive. It features an elegantly furnished club house, with rooms for billiards, cards, TV-viewing and reading; a year-around swimming pool; shuffleboard courts; a therapeutic pool; a deck-lounge area; a fully-equipped kitchen; laundry and car care area.

The streets of Cielo Grande are lighted and there are storage areas for recreational vehicles such as boats and trailers.

Manager's hours at Cielo Grande are from 1 p.m. to 6 p.m. Monday through Friday, and 10 a.m. to 6 p.m. on Saturday and Sunday. Address: 9501 E. Broadway, Mesa, Az 85208. Tel 986-1916.

DESERT SANDS GOLF & COUNTRY CLUB

An adult/retirement mobile home community designed and developed by the Maricopa Realty & Trust Company for mobile home owners on fixed income, the *Desert Sands* community is built around an 18-hole golf course that has an attractive club house. Golf club membership is not mandatory for lot owners.

Address: 7402 E. Baseline Rd., Mesa, Az 85201. Tel 832-6300.

ADULT/RETIREMENT MOBILE HOME PARKS

AMBASSADOR DOWNS—2345 E. Main, Mesa, Az 85203. Tel 964-8315. Heated pool, shuffleboard courts and other recreational facilities. Has mobile homes set up on lot spaces, for sale.

ARIZONA ACRES MOBILE HOME RESORT—9421 E. Apache Trail, Mesa, Az 85207. Tel 986-0220. Monthly and annual rates are available here. Recreational hall, swimming pool, shuffleboard courts and a 9-hole golf course are provided for residents. Mature landscaping.

BRENTWOOD MOBILE MANOR—120 N. Val Vista Dr., Mesa, Az 85203. Tel 832-6260. A large center, Brentwood Manor has a swimming pool, sauna bath, lighted shuffleboard courts, putting green, a 9-hole pitch & put golf course, and laundry facilities. Trailer and boat storage facilities are also available. The park is enclosed, and has a security guard at the entrance.

BROADWAY VISTA MOBILE MANOR--300 S. Val Vista, Mesa, Az 85204. Tel 832-6214. A large park with professional landscaping, fenced perimeters, security guards and sidewalks throughout, the Broadway Vista has both adult and family units. Facilities include a club house and kitchen, laundry rooms, enclosed storage area and refuse containers, game rooms and shuffleboard courts.

CASTILLO NUEVO MOBILE HOME PARK--3300 E. Broadway, Mesa, Az 85204. Tel 832-0802. An adult park that will accept families with children 16 and older, the Castillo Nuevo has swimming and therapeutic pools, outside picnic areas, an exercise room, card and sewing rooms. Utilities are underground.

CITRUS GARDENS MOBILE PARK--4065 E. University Dr., Mesa, Az 85205. Tel 832-0240. From daily to annual rates. Swimming pool, shuffleboard courts and recreation hall. Laundry facilities. There is a golf course a mile away. Large spaces (24") available; models for sale.

COUNTRY COUSINS MOBILE MECCA--61 W. Southern Ave., Mesa, Az 85202. Tel 964-1672. Recreation hall, swimming pool and shuffleboard courts. Trailers for rent.

DESERAMA MOBILE RANCH--2434 E. Main St., Mesa, Az 85203. Tel 964-8850. Swimming pool, recreation hall and shuffleboard courts.

EASTWAY MOBILE PARK--550 E. McKellips Rd., Mesa, Az 85203. Tel 962-0585. Has both adult and family sections, with a swimming pool and laundry facilities. Extra large spaces.

EL MIRAGE MOBILE PARK--305 S. Val Vista, Mesa, Az 85204. Tel 832-0890. A large adult community with single and double-wide spaces, and selection of recreational facilities, including a putting green and therapeutic pool. Laundry.

FOUNTAINS EAST MOBILE HOME PARK--303 S. Recker Rd.,

Mesa, Az 85206. Tel 832-0771. Trailers for rent at
this large, attractive park. Recreation center, pool
and other amenities. Laundry.

HOLIDAY VILLAGE--701 S. Dobson, Mesa, Az 85202.
Tel 962-1694. One of the largest and most attractive
mobile home parks in Mesa, Holiday Village has some
500 permanent mobile home spaces and 83 trailer lots
to accommodate winter visitors. Recreational facilities include a ballroom, arts and crafts room, card
rooms, two swimming pools, a Jacuzzi therapeutic bath,
shuffleboard courts, etc. Planned social events and
other recreational programs feature dances, potluck
dinners and more.

KAY BEE MOBILE VILLA--130 E. McKellips Rd., Mesa,
Az 85201. Tel 969-0611. Has both adult and family
sections, with the usual recreational opportunities
plus two-car parking.

MESA GARDENS TRAILER COURT--1024 W. Main, Mesa, Az
85201. Tel 964-1102. Close to shopping at the large
Tri-City Mall, this small court has a recreation hall
and shuffleboard courts. Bus stops nearby.

MESA VILLAGE MOBILE HOME PARK--2701 E. Allred, Mesa, Az 85204. Tel 969-6062. Has spaces for 12' and
double-widths in a large well-shaded park. Numerous
planned activities, including special dinners on holidays; numerous recreational facilities.

MESA TRAVELODGE MOBILE HOME PARK--253 E. Southern,
Mesa, Az 85202. Tel 969-9222. Mobile homes for rent.
Club room, shuffleboard court and pool.

MON-DAK MOBILE HOME PARK--101 N. 38th St., Mesa,
Az 85206. Tel 832-0430. Recreation center and outdoor
facilities.

PALM GARDENS MOBILE HOME MANOR--2929 E. Main, Mesa,
Az 85203. Tel 832-0290. Large, landscaped lots; tree-
lined paved streets; two separate recreational centers,
including therapy pools. Off-street parking. Planned
social and recreation programs.

PARADISE PALMS TRAILER RESORT--1608 E. Main Street,

Mesa, Az 85203. Tel 964-3552. Recreation center, pool and shuffleboard court.

RAMBLER MOBILE PARK AND APARTMENTS--9225 E. Apache Trail, Mesa, Az 85207. Tel 985-9616. Daily, weekly, monthly and annual rates available. Recreation center and shuffleboard courts.

SUNDIAL MOBILE PARK--2121 N. Center St., Mesa, Az 85201. Tel 969-3621. A large park with a ramada for outside activities in addition to the usual recreational facilities. Laundry.

STEVENSVILLE SUNSET TRAILER PARK--8615 E. Apache Trail, Mesa, Az 85207. Tel 986-1165. A large community with its own golf course, as well as Olympic-sized swimming pool, recreation hall, etc. Regular program of recreation and social activities. Streets are paved and lighted.

TRAILER CITY--730 S. Country Club Dr., Mesa, Az 85202. Tel 964-9350. A small park with adult and family sections. Swimming pool, shuffleboard; laundry facilities.

TRAVEL TRAILER VILLAGE INC--3020 E. Main, Mesa, Az 85203. Tel 832-1770. A huge place with a number of lots for overnight parking. Numerous recreational facilities, including sauna baths.

VENTURE OUT TRAVEL TRAILER RESORT--5001 E. Apache Trail, Mesa, Az 85205. Tel 832-0200. A huge resort-type trailering center with nearly 2,000 spaces, Venture Out has weekly, monthly and yearly rates. Extensive recreational facilities. Trailers for rent.

MINERAL SPRINGS SPA

BUCKHORN MINERAL WELLS
    A few minutes east of downtown Mesa on Apache Trail (Highways 60 & 70), *Buckhorn Mineral Wells* is the only natural hot mineral springs spa in the Valley of the Sun. The spa has furnished apartments and rooms for 100 guests.
    Facilities and services include a modern, spacious

hotsprings bathhouse, whirlpool baths, colonics and
Swedish massage. Expert physiotherapists are also a-
vailable. There is a cafe, post office, beauty salon
and gift shops on the premises. Mailing address is:
P.O. Box 3270, Mesa, Az 85201. Tel (602) 832-1111.

SENIOR CITIZEN GUIDES TO MESA & AREA

The Mesa Chamber of Commerce publishes a monthly
entertainment and recreation guide, especially for
senior citizens, that gives all the needed details
about annual and special events that are of special
interest to retirees and vacationers. The Chamber
also produces a monthly *Sports Calendar* for visitors
and residents, and an up-to-date listing of better
restaurants in the area. The Mesa Chamber of Commerce is at 10 West 1st Street.

Peoria

Peoria is a small community northwest of Phoenix,
between Glendale and Sun City. It is growing and pros-
pering along with Phoenix and all the other cities and
towns in the Valley.

GOOD SHEPHERD RETIREMENT CENTER
LA HACIENDA GOOD SHEPHERD

The adjoining *Good Shepherd Retirement Center* (at
10323 W. Olive, Peoria, Az 85345) and *La Hacienda Good
Shepherd* garden apartments (at 10333 W. Olive) are operated by the Evangelical Luthern Good Samaritan Society, and are exemplary examples of the growing in-
volvement of responsible church organizations in the
needs of the elderly.

The Good Shepherd Retirement Center is a large, in-
clusive facility that combines retirement living and
total nursing care in a home apartment atmosphere. All
services are provided. Residents who are able may come
and go as they please, just as if they were home.

Residency at GSRC is based on a daily charge that

is payable monthly in advance. Optional services are
also available for additional fees.

There are daily recreational and religious activities at GSRC, along with a library, solariums and
hobby rooms. For more details, call 974-2555 or write
to the above address.

La Hacienda Good Shepherd is a large complex of
studio apartments and one-and-two bedroom garden
homes, where convenience, comfort and security in a
loving Christian atmosphere are the bywords.

Residence at La Hacienda is based on a life-time
contract sum plus a monthly service fee. The fee includes monthly housecleaning, janitorial service in
public areas, lawn care, exterior maintenance and
emergency nursing service. Other services available
at additional cost include meals, tray service,
more frequent housecleaning and personal laundry.

For more details about La Hacienda garden apartments write the above address or call 974-8571. Both
Good Shepherd Retirement Center and La Hacienda are
operated under a Resident Bill of Rights that among
other basic rights guarantees privacy for intimate
visits by spouses and friends.

SUN CITY TOWNHOUSE MOBILE ESTATES

At 99th Avenue and Peoria Avenue, immediately adjacent to the eastern boundary of Del E. Webb's Sun
City, *Sun City Townhouse Mobile Estates* is advertis-
ed as America's first townhouse mobile community. Designed especially for adult living, the park is completely enclosed for security. All homes are recess-
ed to ground level so there are no steps, and shopping is just across the street.

The mobile center has a large recreational area
with the usual facilities. Mailing address: 10201 N.
99th Ave., Peoria, Az 85345. Tel 977-1511.

COUNTRY MEADOWS

Adjoining Sun City on the south, *Country Meadows*
is a planned adult community that will eventually
have 2,500 homes on a 642-acre site. The community
includes shopping centers, a large recreation complex
(with pools, tennis courts, etc.), a beautiful golf

course and other amenities.

Housing choices in Country Meadows include apartments as well as two, three and four bedroom homes.
Residency in the adult section of the community is
restricted to persons 35 years old and above, with no
children under 18.

For more details, visit, write or call the developer, Design Master Homes, 105th Avenue & W. Olive Ave.,
Peoria, Az 85345. Tel 933-0116.

Scottsdale

Internationally known for its fabulous resort inns,
guest ranches, hotels, restaurants and fashionable
shops, *Scottsdale* was founded in 1891 by the Reverend
Winfield Scott as a health community. The tiny settlement remained in the shadow of Phoenix for several decades, then began to blossom as a center for arts and
crafts; finally becoming a plush resort city noted for
its Western motif.

Today Scottsdale is one of the largest cities in
the state, serving as a residential area for people
who work in all parts of the Valley, as well as a maj-
or year-around attraction for tourists, conventioneers,
vacationers and retirees.

Set in between Phoenix on the west, the Salt River
Indian Reservation on the east, and Tempe of the south,
Scottsdale is now growing northward towards the foothills of the McDowell Mountains. Since it is primarily
a residential/resort city with the accent on luxurious
living and playing in the sun, Scottsdale is unusually
attractive even by Arizona standards.

Following the pattern set by the first large resorts to locate in the area, most of the commercial
businesses, home and apartment builders have maintained the plushy Spanish-Indian-Mexican-Western architectural flavor that has become Scottsdale's trademark.

Although Scottsdale is attracting more retired residents on a year-around basis, the city at this point
is of primary interest to those who are quite affluent

and who select it as a place to spend their winter
months. While only a few car-minutes from downtown
Phoenix, Scottsdale seems to have an even better climate than its larger neighbor--and definitely less
man-made pollution. Many of the businesses as well
as social and cultural activities reach their peak
during the winter months.

Among the Scottsdale resorts that attract many
affluent retirees during the winter season are Camelback Inn on the slopes of Mummy Mountain, Casa Blanca
Inn on the eastern slopes of Camelback Mountain,
Mountain Shadows Resort Hotel and Country Club on the
northern waist of Camelback Mountain, the Safari Hotel, Sunburst Hotel, Hilton Hotel, Ride-N-Rock Ranch,
Scottsdale Inn & Country Club and the Valley Ho Hotel.

Then there are a large number of apartments, lodges,
motels and ranches that cater to long-term winter
guests. These include The Bunkhouse Lodge; the Hitch-
ing Post Motel & Apartments; Lantron's Court; OutPost
Lodge & Inn; Paradise Valley Guest Ranch; Sahauro
Lake Guest Ranch (25 miles northeast of Scottsdale in
the Tonto National Forest); Shangri La Guest Ranch
and Yellow Boot Ranch.

All of the above are resort and vacation facilities,
and do not cater in any particular way to those who
have retired. There are a number of housing facilities in Scottsdale that are designed specifically for
adult and/or retirement living, however. These include:

SCOTTSDALE NEW VENTURA

A large complex of garden apartments, with handicapped and health service units, the *New Ventura* provides meals and maid service, security, transportation and planned recreational activities. Facilities
include a swimming pool, beauty parlor, laundary and
garden plots. Address: 980 N. Granite Reef Rd., Scottsdale, Az 85257. Tel 949-9086

SCOTTSDALE SHADOWS

A forerunner of what living may be like for the majority of Americans some time in the future, *Scottsdale Shadows* might be described as a "total apartment

community," A project of Environmental Developers of
Denver (an affiliate of Trans-Union Corporation), on
Camelback Road between 78th Street and Hayden Road,
Scottsdale Shadows is a 40-acre complex that consists
of 13 highrise condominium apartment buildings and a
large recreational building--all surrounded by a 9-
hole golf course, three swimming pools, tennis courts
and green park areas.

The special attraction of Scottsdale Shadows, in
which residency is limited to adults 39 or older with
no children under 16, is that its concept and design
puts the convenience, comfort and pleasure of the occupants first. The developers call it their "total
environment concept."

Use of the Community Center at Scottsdale Shadows
includes the swimming pools, sauna baths, exercise
rooms, party rooms, kitchen facilities, shuttle bus,
picnic areas, classes in hobbies, crafts and langua-
ges; plus free attendance at lectures, cultural e-
vents and more.

Some of the special features that go with the condominium apartments: built-in TV antennas; large sliding glass doors to individual, secluded lanais; con-
tinuous fresh air ventilation that is exhausted through the bath duct; individual apartment air-conditioning; extra electrical outlets; storage lockers;
laundry rooms; trash chutes down the hallway from
each apartment; a security lock on the building entrance which opens only when an occupant pushes a
release button; armed security guards; and underground parking to keep cars safe all the time and
cool during the summer months.

Scottsdale Shadows was designed by the famous a-
ward-winning architect Bennie Gonzalez. Among the in-
novations he built into the adult-styled apartments:
walls designed to be acoustically dead and therefore
soundproof; and 8-inch thick steel-reinforced concrete floors to keep noises from going up and down.

For more information contact Scottsdale Shadows,
7800 E. Camelback Rd., Scottsdale, Az 85251. Tel
994-0333.

SCOTTSDALE VILLAGE SQUARE

A large garden apartment complex, with separate courtyards, that includes a personal health-care center, *Scottsdale Village Square* is designed specifically for active senior adults.

One-bedroom unfurnished apartments are leased on a yearly basis. The lease fee includes two meals daily, weekly maid service and use of all the facilities. All apartments have emergency call and intercom systems. Amenities include a swimming pool and Jacuzzi bath; a dining-social center; an arts and crafts center; a barber and beauty shop. A large shopping center adjoins.

Scottsdale Village Square is at 2620 N. 68th St., Scottsdale, Az 85257. Tel 946-6571.

VILLA OCTILLO

Another plush retirement apartment complex, with "catered" services, *Villa Octillo* offers a choice of suites, private rooms and semi-private rooms. Services include three meals a day, coffee and tea hours and maid service. An attendant is on duty 24-hours a day, and there are planned recreational activities. Other amenities: a swimming pool, library, recreation lounge and beauty shop. Address: 3327 N. Civic Center Plaza, Scottsdale, Az 85251. Tel 945-2637.

KAISER AETNA MCCORMICK RANCH

Scottsdale's famous *McCormick Ranch*, bought by Kaisner Aetna in 1970, is being developed—in a five-phase 15-year program—into a master-planned community that will have several features of special interest to adult couples and retirees who are relatively affluent.

The huge 4,200-acre ranch, overlooking the mamestic McDowell Mountains to the northeast and Camelback Mountain to the west (and entirely within the city limits of Scottsdale) is being turned into a series of contiguous communities designed to preserve the character of the land and diminish the role of the automobile. Openness of space, horse trails,

pedestrian walks, bicycle paths, golf courses and several lakes are prime features of the project. The
different village communities and resort facilities
within the Ranch are linked together by a band of
open space called *Camelback Walk*, which in some areas
is 300 feet wide.

Homesites and a variety of homestyles, including
two and three-bedroom condominiums, villas and hacien-
das, are offered in the first of the ranch properties
to be developed. Also of special interest to well-to-
do senior citizens is the Ranch's *Resort Village* on
the southwest side of the property. Winter visitors
and short-term vacationers who put up in the village
can take advantage of two 18-hole golf course, a complete tennis center, swimming pools, sailing facilities, an esquestrian center, and more.

For details, visit or write: McCormick Ranch Information Center, 7350 N. Hayden Rd., Scottsdale, Az
85253. Tel 948-4030.

ADULT/RETIREMENT MOBILE HOME COMMUNITIES

PUEBLO SERENO
A large, elaborate community with a country-club
like atmosphere, *Pueblo Sereno* has several lake-view
spaces. Among the facilities: a large club house;
swimming pool; Jacuzzi therapeutic pool; billiards
room; laundry room; storage space; and a recreation
vehicle for use by residents.

The community also has its own fishing lake with
electric boats available; and a putting green. Social
and recreational activities are planned. The Pueblo
is at 8350 E. McKellips Rd. Tel 946-4205.

SCOTTSDALE ROADRUNNER LAKE RESORT
A huge place with resort-type facilities, the
Scottsdale Roadrunner Lake Resort is reserved for
adults-only during winter months. Besides a large,
well-equipped Recreation Center, the mobile home resort has an Olympic-sized pool and two Jacuzzi therapeutic baths. Pads measure 33'x53'.

The Roadrunner is on Roadrunner Blvd., (off 92nd

St. south of McDowell Rd.), Scottsdale, Az 85252. Tel
945-0787.

MOBILE HOME PARKS

WHEEL INN TRAILER RANCH--7010 E. Continental Dr.,
Scottsdale, Az 85257. Tel 945-7491. Within walking
distance to shopping, this attractive trailer park has
the usual recreational facilities, and is within a few
minutes of three championship golf courses.

RIVIERA MOBILE HOME PARK--601 N. Hayden Rd., Scottsdale, Az 85257. Tel 947-6261. An adult part with 200
spaces for permanent residents and 14 lots for travel trailers, the Riviera has an unusually attractive
recreation area, and publishes a monthly program for
its tenants. The park also has its own coffee shop.

HACIENDA DE LOS ARCOS
Sponsored by the Los Arcos United Methodist Church
congregation, the *Hacienda de los Arcos* consists of
125 apartments in nine 2-story buildings. Twenty-nine
of the apartments are leased at reduced rates to tenants who qualify for a federal rental supplement. All
of the apartments are rented on an equal opportunity
basis. Residents must be 62 or over and qualify for
low-cost housing.
The nine buildings in the center are roughly "U"
shaped, face opposite directions to avoid regimentation, and are spaced far apart. A central building
houses the manager's office, a recreation room, a
snack bar, TV lounge, arts and crafts rooms, a reading
room, and laundry facilities.
For details, contact Hacienda de los Arcos, 7529
E. Culver St., Scottsdale, Az 85257. Tel 945-4991.

Tempe

Tempe, adjacent to Phoenix on the southeast, is a
large and growing city in its own right, but like Glendale on the west is practically an extension of Phoe-

nix. Long known as a "sleepy little college town,"
Tempe is now much more than that.

The heart of Tempe is *Arizona State University,*
one of the great universities in the country. Its cultural and sports functions, as well as its economic im-
pact, are a major factor thoughout the Valley of the
Sun.

Most of the retired population in Tempe live in
conventional homes and apartments. But there are several facilities in Tempe that are designed for retirement living.

FRIENDSHIP VILLAGE

Situated on a 45-acre site in beautiful south Tempe
near Desert Samaritan Hospital, *Friendship Village* is
one of the most attractive life-care retirement facilities in the state. In addition to apartments and
garden cottages, it features a health center, and offers a broad range of social, recreational, cultural
and religious activities.

Life-care endowments and a monthly fee cover the
use of the 24-hour health center, which provides one
meal a day plus nursing care as long as it is needed.
All outside maintenance is taken care of, and there
is maid and laundry service

The garden homes are at 2625 E. Southern Avenue.
The highrise apartment building is at 2645 E. Southern.
For detailed information about residency in the village, write or visit: Friendship Village, 600 E. Baseline Rd (a model apartment), Tempe, Az 85283. Tel
831-5000.

MOBILE HOME PARKS

THE MEADOWS--2401 W. Southern Ave., Tempe. Tel
967-9461. A luxurious adult mobile home community,
the Meadows has the usual array of recreational facilities.

TEMPE CASCADE MOBILE HOME COMMUNITY--2340 E. University Dr., Tempe. Tel 968-3263. Has both adult and
family sections, with a full range of recreational facilities.

RANCHO RIO VISTA MOBILE HOME PARK--1820 W. University Dr., Tempe. Tel 966-2141. Adults only. Laundry facilities, shuffleboard.

RETIREES OF TEMPE ASSOCIATION
   Among the agencies and activities of special interest to senior citizens in Tempe is the *Retirees of Tempe Association,* sponsored by the City of Tempe and coordinated by the Parks and Recreation Department. The Association offers retirees a full range of social and recreational opportunities, including shopping trips, potluck dinners, community work, etc.
   Membership in the Association costs $1 a year, but its activities are open to all senior citizens whether or not they are members. Anyone interested in the Association should call the Retired Citizens' Coordinator at the Tempe Community Center (Rural Road and Southern Avenue), at 968-8387.
   Tempe also has a chapter of the *American Association of Retired Persons,* which meets the second Friday of every month at the Tempe Community Center, 3500 S. Rural Road. A *Retired Senior Volunteer Program,* which serves Mesa and Scottsdale as well as Tempe, is sponsored by the Mesa Community College.
   Tempe also has a *Meals-on-Wheels* program which delivers meals to older people who live alone and cannot fix their own meals. The program is headquartered at the Tempe Community Hospital, where the meals are prepared.
   For more details about the meal program or any other matter relating to retirees in the Tempe area, contact the Retired Citizens' Coordinator.
   Tempe's Parks and Recreation Department sponsors group meetings of senior citizens at the Civic Center several times a month.

OTHER RETIREMENT COMMUNITIES
IN OR NEAR THE VALLEY OF THE SUN**

AHWATUKEE

There are a number of retirement and planned com-

munities outside the urban areas of Greater Phoenix
but within or near the Valley of the Sun that are also
of special interest.

One of these communities is *Ahwatukee,* a 2,500-acre
planned retirement center located off the I-10 Freeway
just south of Baseline Road, near Tempe.

The retirement living section of Ahwatukee is separate from the family living development, and offers
single unit homes, townhouses, villas and duplexes.
They include carpet, convenience kitchens, covered patios, air-conditioning, underground utilities. Exterior maintenance is provided for townhouses and duplexes. Some models feature cathedral ceilings and
wood-burning fireplaces.

There is a large Retirement Recreation Center that
has a pool, a ballroom with kitchen facilities for
parties, shuffleboard courts, lawn bowling, a Jacuzzi
and sauna bath, exercise rooms, arts and crafts rooms,
etc.

There is also a luxurious country club that boasts
a championship golf course and 14 lighted tennis
courts.

For more information about this extraordinary development, contact the Ahwatukee Sales Office, 11218
Beaver Tail Dr., Phoenix, Az 85044. Tel 893-2646.

FLORENCE

Approximately equi-distant from Phoenix/Scottsdale
and Tucson on Arizona Highways 80 and 89, *Florence* is
a desert community that enjoys the same bright sunshine and mild climate of the Valley of the Sun cities
but has none of the heavy traffic or pollution and
none of the other disadvantages usually associated
with big-city living.

Situated in an area that is unusually picturesque
and colorful--even for Arizona--Florence has two major
facilities catering to winter vacationeers and retirees.

FLORENCE GARDENS--A distinctive mobile home center,

Florence Gardens offers its residents a wide range of
recreational facilities and other amenities, from a
golf course and club house to city trash pick-up.
For current rates, write or call Western American Communities, 600 Gila Blvd., Florence, Az 85232. Tel 868-
5583.

CALIENTE CASA DE SOL--An adult travel trailer and
RV resort, Caliente Casa de Sol is a member of the
Good Sampark system, which assures its residents and
visitors of high standards. Facilities here include
modern restrooms with showers, year-around swimming
pools, therapeutic pools, sauna baths, a golf course
and more.
For other information and reservations, call or
write Caliente Casa de Sol, Star Route One, Florence,
Az 85232. Tel 868-5520.

FOUNTAIN HILLS

Not specifically a retirement community, but a
planned city of extraordinary interest to all ages
and categories, *Fountain Hills* is a city of the future being built for today.

A project of the very successful McCulloch Development Company which built Lake Havasu City, Fountain Hills is taking shape on the rolling eastern
slopes of the McDowell Mountains, 19 miles northeast of downtown Scottsdale and 30 miles northeast
of downtown Phoenix, overlooking the Verde River.

Fountain Hills has several keys that should insure its success and eventually make it one of the
showplaces of the state. Over and above the scenic
grandeur of its location is the fact that it is
isolated from but within 30 to 40 minutes of virtually any destination in Greater Phoenix--and
even closer to the state's most popular recreational lake and mountain country.

From Fountain Hills via Apache Trail, Saguaro
Lake (the first of a chain of Salt River lakes)
is only 12 miles away. Canyon Lake is only 47
miles away; Apache Lake is 62 miles, and the huge
Roosevelt Lake is just 80 miles away. Two other

lakes on the nearby Verde River, Bartlett and Horseshoe, are 48 and 51 miles respectively from Fountain
Hills.

A third key is the fact that Fountain Hills is planned to be a balanced, self-contained community with
built-in controls to avoid the problems that now plag-
ue big cities. Programmed to have a maximum population
of 70,000, which is less than six persons per acre, as
compared to the 40 to 80 persons per acre in most old
cities, Fountain Hills is divided into 11 districts.

When the city is fully completed, these districts
will be made up of four residential areas: neighborhood shopping complexes; urban shopping centers; general commercial districts (hotels/motels, light industries); parks and greenbelts; and schools. The
open park areas contain a large man-made lake, three
golf courses and horse trails.

A fourth key in the Fountain Hills master plan is
that architectural control is exercised on the design and construction of all buildings--residential,
commercial and industrial; and the developers are
charged with the responsibility not only of maintain-
ing the natural beauty of the area but adding to it.

A fifth key that will go a long way toward pro-
tecting Fountain Hills from the blight of urban sprawl
and oversize is that it cannot grow mushroom style.
Adjoining the community on the north is the McDowell
Mountain Regional Park. On the south and east lie
large Indian Reservations. The rugged McDowell Mountains stand to the west.

The philosophy of Fountain Hills is described as
providing the "openness and beauty of a rural atmosphere within a city;" along with mechanisms that will
prevent the core of the city from deteriorating with
growth and age.

To reach Fountain Hills, drive east on Shea Boulevard from Phoenix or Scottsdale; or northeast on Beeline Highway, from McDowell Road, east of Scottsdale.
You can see the symbol of the community before you
get there--a column of snow-white water that jets up
560 feet into the air from the center of a lake. For

information about homesites in Fountain Hills, contact the Sales Office, 12065 N. Saguaro Blvd., Fountain Hills, Az 85268. Tel 837-9890.

QUEEN VALLEY

Fifteen miles east of Apache Junction (and about an hour's drive from Phoenix) in the foothills of the Superstition Mountains, *Queen Valley* is a closed-in secluded oasis that has a special appeal for those who want to get away from the hubbub and hurrying of modernday urban life. The Valley, with a cool, clear creek and natural springs, was a favorite camping grounds for Arizona Indians from earliest times. The Spaniards also used the small basin-like valley as a source of water and grass when they were mining gold in the Superstitions during the 1600s and 1700s.

Part of the attraction of Queen Valley is that it appears like a huge, natural amphitheater, with most of the green floor taken up by an 18-hole golf course, several ponds, a swimming pool and a number of other recreational facilities.

One side of the Valley is devoted to mobile homes; the other side to conventional homes. Nearly all of the homes of both sides of the Valley have superb panoramic views of the valley floor and the surrounding mountains. To preserve the naturalness of the scene, all utilities are underground.

To reach Queen Valley from the Phoenix area, drive east on U.S. Highways 60/70, going through Mesa, Apache Junction and Florence Junction. Just beyond Florence Junction turn north onto Whitlow Dam Road. The Valley is only a short drive from the main highway, over rolling desert foothills.

SUN LAKES

Sun Lakes is one of the most popular retirement areas in the Valley of the Sun. Located 13 miles south of Tempe off the I-10 Freeway, Sun Lakes is not totally a retirement community. Many of the residents work full-time, but the atmosphere is leisure, fun oriented and for adults only. One property owner must

be at least 40 years of age, with no full-time residents under the age of 19. Children and grandchild-
ren are welcomed and encouraged to visit.

Membership in the Sun Lakes Country Club comes
with property purchase, and Sun Lakes offers conventional housing as well as mobile home living. Lots
for mobile homes are purchased, and while there is a
mobile home sales office on the location, it is not
required that the homes be purchased from the developer.

All utilities at Sun Lakes are underground and all
sites are furnished with central water systems, sewerage systems, natural gas and a 20-channel, two-way
cable television system. The community has its own
fire and security protection 24 hours a day, seven
days a week.

Recreational facilities at Sun Lakes include an
18-hole golf course and pro shop with a PGA golf pro
in attendance full time; a huge double-level heated
swimming pool; an indoor/outdoor pool; a Jacuzzi
whirlpool; lighted tennis and paddle tennis courts;
health studios, including sauna baths; shuffleboard
and horseshoe pits; bicycle, walking and golf-cart
paths; gas barbecues and lounge areas. Monthly dues
are nominal.

Sun Lakes offers name entertainment in the winter
months, and sponsors luaus, Mexican fiestas, costume
balls, and Christmas and New Year's parties. A small
neighboring shopping center with additional specialty
shops is avilable to residents.

For a brochure and other information about Sun
Lakes, write or call: Sun Lakes, 256601 Sun Lakes
Blvd., Sun Lakes, Az 85224. Tel (602) 963-6335.

PARADISE VALLEY

CAMELBACK MANOR
Nestled on the waist of Camelback Mountain between Scottsdale and Phoenix, *Camelback Manor Lodge*
is a retirement home for elderly affluent ladies. The
monthly fee includes home-cooked meals, personal laundry, help with bathing, companionship, TLC and

supervision. Camelback Manor Lodge is at 6030 Camelback Manor Dr., Paradise Valley, Az 85253. Tel 959-
8676.

III

SPECIAL AGENCIES & SERVICES FOR RETIREES IN THE VALLEY OF THE SUN

There are many agencies and organizations in the Valley of the Sun—on federal, state, city and private levels—whose purpose is to serve the interests and needs of senior citizens directly or to help them indirectly by promoting desirable legislation and other means. These include the following:

ADELANTE CON MESA

Established under the auspices of the Office of Economic Opportunity, *Adelante Con Mesa* or Forward With Mesa (and other surrounding communities, including Apache Junction), offers a number of services of interest to the less affluent elderly, and also serves as an information and referral center for all the services of the community.

The agency is in the Tri-City Multi-Services Building, 21 S. Hibbert, Mesa. Tel 834-7777, Ext. 334 or 335. Calls from retired persons are welcomed.

ADULT & SENIOR CITIZEN CENTERS

Senior and adult centers are playing an increasingly important role in the lives of retirees in Arizona, not only as sources of information and education, but also as sources of companionship and recreational opportunities.

The following list covers centers in the Valley of the Sun. For those in other areas, see the appropriate sections and a follow-up list in the back of this book.

CASA GRANDE

CASA GRANDE SENIOR CENTER--306 E. 6th St. Tel 836-9059. Open 8 .m. to 5 p.m. weekdays. Arts and crafts; continuing educational programs. Golf on Mondays; potluck dinners on Wednesdays.

CHANDLER

CHANDLER GOLDEN AGE CENTER--32 E. Buffalo. Tel 963-3542. Open weekdays form 8:30 to 4 p.m., with activities ranging from movies to bingo. Shopping bus on Saturdays.

EL MIRAGE

TWIN CITIES SENIOR CENTER--14010 E. Mirage Rd. Tel 583-0519. Hours: 8 a.m. to 4 p.m. Noon meals plus a variety of social and recreational activities.

GLENDALE

SENIOR CITIZEN'S CLUB (Community Bldg.)--7022 N. 58th Dr. Tel 931-5585. Meets Monday at 11:30 a.m. for potluck lunch and cards.

SENIOR CITIZEN'S CRAFT CLUB (Community Bldg.)--7022 N. 58th Dr. Tel 931-5585. Meets Wednesday at 10 a.m. for crafts and social activities.

YWCA NUTRITION PROGRAM--6242 N. 59th Ave. Tel 937-4273. Open weekdays from 10 a.m. to 2 p.m. Noon meals plus social events.

MESA

EAST MESA SENIOR CENTER--310 N. 73rd St. Tel 985-9803. Hours: 8 a.m. to 4 p.m. weekdays. Crafts, entertainment and educational programs.

MESA SENIOR CENTER--264 N. Center. Tel 964-1321. Open from 8 a.m. to 4 p.m. weekdays. Speakers, other programs and activities.

PHOENIX

ALDERSGATE NUTRITION SITE--3530 N. 32nd St. Tel

262-7807. Crafts, games, educational programs, recreation, blood-pressure checks.

BETHEL CENTER--7th St. & Osborn. Tel 262-6411. Arts, crafts, games, movies, open forum; blood-pressure checks. Open 10 a.m. to 2 p.m. weekdays.

CAMPBELL NUTRITION SITE--37th Ave & Campbell. Tel 262-4779. Hours: 10 a.m. to 2 p.m. Noon meals, ceramics, games, group discussions.

CAPITOL SENIOR CITIZENS CENTER--1604 W. Van Buren. Tel 253-3443. Noon meals and numerous social and recreational activities. Shopping trips.

COFFELT NUTRITION SITE--1943 W. Pima. Tel 262-7354. Open 10 a.m. to 2 p.m. Noon meals, recreation and educational programs.

JEWISH COMMUNITY CENTER--1718 W. Maryland. Tel 249-1832. Noon meals; numerous social and recreational activities. Transportation to and from the center.

LUKE-KROHN SENIOR CENTER--904½ E. Villa. Tel 262-6835. Open 8:30 a.m. to 4:30 p.m. weekdays. Lunch, games and recreation, service programs, shopping trips.

MARCOS DE NIZA SENIOR CENTER--303 W. Pima. Tel 262-7249. Open 8:30 to 4:30 weekdays. Breakfast on Monday, Wednesday and Friday; lunches daily. Recreational ans social activities.

NORTH PHOENIX ADULT CENTER--2240 W. Citrus Way. Tel 262-4791. One of the most attractive, most popular and successful adult centers in Arizona. Housed in beautiful quarters just west of the *Phoenix Tennis Center*, it provides a wide variety of recreational, social and cultural events Monday thru Saturday. Open from 9:30 a.m. to 10 p.m. on weekdays, from noon to 4:30 p.m. on Saturdays, and from 1 p.m. to 5 p.m. on Sundays. Facilities include a beautiful lounge, library, auditorium, card and craft rooms and meeting rooms.

NORTHWEST SENIOR CENTER--13001 N. 35th Ave. Tel

262-4791. Noon meals, games, classes and speakers.

OKEMA SENIOR CENTER--1728 E. Pueblo. Tel 276-5127. Open from 8:30 a.m. to 4:30 p.m. on weekdays. Lunch, exercise programs, classes and games.

OSBORN SENIOR CENTER--806 W. Osborn. Tel 274-3398. Open week days from 8:30 a.m. Crafts, games, field trips, shopping, counseling and referral services.

ST. FRANCIS ADULT GROUP (Xavier Hall)--4715 N. Central Ave. Tel 265-3916. Crafts, games, social events and business meetings.

ST. PAUL'S NUTRITION SITE--149 N. 28th Ave. Tel 261-8951. Open 9 a.m. to 1 p.m. on weekdays. Lunch, crafts, games, shopping trips and speaker programs.

SALVATION ARMY SENIOR CITIZEN WALK-IN CENTER--612 N. 3rd Ave. Tel 254-5187. Open 8 to 5 weekdays; 9 to 4 Saturdays; noon to 4 on Sundays. Lunch, educational programs, recreation, transportation and blood-pressure checks.

SENIOR OPPORTUNITIES WEST--1326 W. Hadley. Tel 262-6610. Open 8:30 to 4:30 weekdays. Serves breakfast and lunch. Exercise programs.

SENIOR SERVICES EAST--1417 E. Mohave. Tel 262-7305. Open from 8:30 to 4:30. Lunch served on weekdays. Arts and crafts, exercise programs and classes daily.

SOUTH PHOENIX ADULT CENTER--212 E. Alta Vista. Tel 262-4093. Open weekdays from 9:30 a.m. to 10 p.m.; also on Saturdays from 10 a.m. to 2 p.m. and Sundays from 1 p.m. to 5 p.m. Numerous educational, social and recreational activities in a very attractive center.

SUNNYSLOPE SENIOR CENTER--9317 N. 2nd St. Tel 997-6811. Open 8:30 a.m. to 4:30 p.m. Lunch served on weekdays. Exercise classes, games and shopping trips.

WASHINGTON MANOR--1123 E. Monroe. Tel 261-8816. Lunch program, arts and crafts, exercise classes

swimming, other recreational activities and social
events.

"Y" NUTRITION PROGRAM--2602 E. Clarendon. Tel
261-8578. Open 10 a.m. to 2 p.m. weekdays. Lunch
program, swimming, games, movies and speakers.

YWCA NUTRITION PROGRAM--230 E. Earll. Tel 264-
3811. Open from 11 a.m. to 3 p.m. weekdays. Lunch
and educational programs, recreation, entertainment,
information and referral service.

SCOTTSDALE

SCOTTSDALE SENIOR CENTER--7375 E. 2nd St., Tel
994-2375. Open weekdays from 10 a.m. to 5 p.m.;
Saturdays from noon until 5 p.m. and then again
from 7:30 p.m. to 11 p.m. for a dance; on Sundays
from noon until 5 p.m. Wide variety of recreational,
educational and social activities, in an attractive
center.

VISTA DEL CAMINO SERVICE CENTER--7700 E. Roosevelt. Tel 994-2323, ext. 23. Open daily from 8 a.m.
Nutrition program, health services, legal aid and
economic aid.

TEMPE

ESCALANTE CENTER--2150 E. Orange. Tel 966-8867.
Open 8 a.m. to 4 p.m. weekdays. Lunch plus numerous
recreational opportunities, including swimming.

TEMPE COMMUNITY CENTER--3500 S. Rural Rd. Tel
968-8387. Open from 8:30 a.m. to 10 p.m. on weekdays, and from 9 a.m. to 5 p.m. on Saturdays. Numerous social, recreational and education programs in
an attractive setting.

OTHER SENIOR SERVICE CENTERS

PRESBYTERIAN SERVICE CENTER

The *Presbyterian Service Center,* at 34 E. Roeser
Rd., Phoenix, is a "drop-in" facility for senior
citizens. It provides counseling, self-help programs

and recreation, plus opportunities to do community work. Two senior citizen clubs meet at the Center. Tel 268-6836.

ALCOHOL PROBLEMS

ALCOHOL CRISIS INTERVENTION
   Operated by the Phoenix Alcohol Safety Action Program and LEAP, the ACI sponsors a telephone hot-line counseling service for people with alcohol problems. Number to call is 258-8011. The center also provides transportation assistance for problem drinkers.
   Other agencies concered with alcoholism include the Arizona Recovery Centers Association (258-5373); Alcoholism Information Center (264-6214) at 1525 E. Osborn Road in Phoenix, and Alcoholics Anonymous (264-1341).

ANIMALS

   ARIZONA ANIMAL WELFARE LEAGUE--1118 E. Indian School Rd., Phoenix, Az. 85014. Tel 956-9498. Provides low-cost neutering and spaying.

   ARIZONA HUMANE SOCIETY--9226 N. 13th Ave., Phoenix, Az 85021. Tel 997-7588. Animal protection and adoption.

   PET-LINE--4550 W. Glenn Dr., Glendale, Az 85301. Tel 269-1391. Lost-and-found liasion service, adoption and tattooing.

   VETERINARY SAMARITAN PROGRAM--6040 N. 7th St., Phoeniz Az 85014. Tel 274-4659. Free spaying and neutering of pets for people on social security and other fixed low incomes.

ANNUAL AUTO INSPECTIONS

   All cars less than 10 years old must pass annual inspections (for pollution control) in order to be registered and licensed in Arizona. Call the inspection station nearest you for current operating hours:

   Mesa, 1830 W. Broadway.............. 969-9859

Phoenix, 8802 N. Black Canyon Freeway.. 955-5088
Phoenix, 12620 N. Cave Creek Rd..... 971-7640
Phoenix, 2450 S. 7th St............ 258-0395
Phoenix, 4501 W. Van Buren.......... 269-2094
Scottsdale, 1700 N. Hayden Rd....... 945-7325

If you have a complaint about auto repairs done by garages, contact the Automobile Service Council, 14 S. 41st Pl., Phoenix, Az 85034. Tel 275-6293. Complaints about used cars should be referred to the Arizona Independent Auto Dealers Association, 1433 N. 3rd Ave., Phoenix, Az 85003. Tel 257-1232.

ARTS & CRAFTS

The *Senior Citizen's Arts & Crafts Center,* Camelot Shops, 914 E. Camelback Rd., Phoenix, provides senior citizens with an opportunity to sell their hand-made items to supplement their incomes. Tel 266-0145.

Mesa Activity Arts & Crafts, 155 N. Center Ave., in Mesa also sells arts and crafts made by senior citizens. For information about getting into arts and crafts as a past-time or money-making enterprise, contact the *Art Barn,* City of Mesa, Parks & Recreation Dept., 125 N. Hobson, Mesa. Tel 834-2308.

BLIND SERVICES

There are a number of facilities offering services for the blind in Maricopa County. These includes the following:

Alpha Omega, 821 N. 3rd St., Phoenix, Az 85004. Tel 257-8884. This agency assesses the needs of blind, disabled and aged persons in their homes, and seeks to meet these needs directly or refers them to the appropriate agency.

Arizona Low Vision Services Inc., 1016 N. 32nd St., Phoenix, Az 85008. Tel 275-3723. ALVSI helps the nearly blind maintain their independence and cope with daily living. Call only on Thursdays.

Guide Dogs for the Blind, P.O. Box 206, Scottsdale, Az 85252. Tel 948-5480. This group provides in-residence training programs for legally blind adults and suitable guide dogs.

Of special interest to the blind and disabled is the *Arizona Regional Library for the Blind and Physically Handicapped,* at 1036 N. 32nd St., Phoenix, tel 271-5578. The library offers the visually impaired and those unable to hold a book or turn the pages free "talking books" and equipment, such as record players, cassette tape recorders, earphones, speed and remote control units, etc.

After an individual registers with the library, the selection of books in braille and on tapes and records can be made by mail with no postal charge for receiving or returning the materials. Call the above number for information on how to register.

BLOOD-PRESSURE TESTING

There are several locations in Maricopa County where you can get your blood-pressure checked free. Call the American Heart Association, tel 277-4846, for the site nearest you.

BUREAU OF HEARINGS & APPEALS

This is the agency of the Social Security Administration that conducts hearings on Social Security claims that have been denied at a lower level. The agency is at 3033 N. Central Ave., Phoenix. Hours are 8 a.m. to 4:30 p.m. Tel 261-3828.

CAMELBACK HOSPITAL COUNSELINE

This is a tape library of free information, professionally prepared to help any caller understand more about life's most challenging problems (dying, death, alcohol and other drugs, tension, sexuality and sexual roles, emotional problems, etc.)--and is one of the most successful telephone counseling services in the state.

The program is jointly operated by Camelback Hospital, CB Mental Health Center and Scottsdale Camelback Hospital, and is available to anyone in Arizona from 10 a.m. to 7 p.m. every weekday.

Altogether there are 50 tapes in 11 vital areas.

Each tape is identifed by a number listed in a brochure. To obtain a copy of the brochure call the
Counseline operator at 994-8499 and ask that one be
sent to you by mail, or pick one up at a senior or
adult center in the area.

To use the service, just dial the Counseline number and give the code number of the tape you want to
hear. If you do not have the number, give the subject
you are interested in.

COMMUNITY COUNCIL

The *Community Council* is a funded organization designed to promote and help develop an efficient and
effective community program of health, welfare, recreation and educational services through the voluntary participations of citizens, agencies and social
organizations.

The Council also operates an *Information & Referral Service* that maintains files on the health, education, recreation and welfare resources of Maricopa
County, and undertakes to help individuals and groups
select the community services that will best meet
their needs.

The Community Council is at 1515 E. Osborn Rd.,
Phoenix. Tel 263-8853. Hours are 8:30 a.m. to 5 p.m.
on weekdays.

CONSUMER PROTECTION

There are several dozen local and federal agencies
where you may lodge complaints about faulty products
and services. These include the following (The telephone numbers listed are mostly for the Phoenix/
Scottsdale/Tempe/Mesa area. In Tucson and other cities see the appropriate listing in the Telephone Directory or call the local Information & Referral Service).*

APPLIANCES--The Electric League of Arizona, at
263-9391, accepts complaints about sales and service
on most electricial appliances, heating and cooling
units, and home-insulation products. The league does
<u>not</u> accept complaints about television or stereo

equipment and repairs. League officials will advise shoppers on which electrical products and services are best suited to their homes and needs.

AUTOMOBILES--The Arizona Automobile Dealers Association, tel 252-2386, tries to resolve customer complaints against its members, which include almost all new-car dealers in the state. Under a nationally sponsored dealers' program, the association works closely with the county attorney's economic crimes division at 261-5831. If you suspect that the odometer on a used car has been rolled back, notify the FBI at 279-5511. For suspected safety defects, call the U.S. Department of Transportation on the toll-free number 800-424-9393. For complaints about used card dealers who do not belong to the AADA, call the Better Business Bureau at 264-1721.

BANKS--The state Banking Department handles complaints against state-chartered banks, savings and loan associations, finance companies, mortgage brokers, collection agencies, escrow companies, title companies and trust companies. Tel 255-4421.

Complaints against federally chartered banks go to the U.S. Comptroller of Currency, with regional offices in Denver, (303) 837-4883. Complaints about a federally chartered savings and loan association go to the Federal Home Loan Bank Board in San Francisco, (415) 393-1000. The state Banking Department will advise you on which agency has jurisdiction over a particular banking institution.

BARBERS--Barbershops are licensed and regulated by the state Board of Barber Examiners, and complaints should be lodged with that agency, 255-4498.

BEAUTY SHOPS--Complaints should be made to the state Board of Cosmetology, at 255-5301.

CONSTRUCTION--The state Registrar of Contractors at 255-1511 investigates complaints against building contractors and sub-contractors such as electricians, plumbers, cement masons, carpenters, roofers, painters and swimming pool builders.

CREDIT--For information about bank loans and credit cards issued by banks, call the state Banking Department at 255-4421. For complaints about credit discrimination, credit report confidentiality and fair collection practices, call the Los Angeles office of the Federal Trade Commission, (213) 824-7575.

DRUGS--Problems about prescription drugs are handled by the U.S. Food and Drug Administration, at 261-3280. Complaints about non-prescription drugs should go to the Federal Trade Comission in L.A. (213) 824-7575.

EMPLOYMENT AGENCIES--Businesses that promise or seek to obtain employment for persons in exchange for a fee are regulated by the state Labor Department, at 255-4515.

ENERGY-SAVING DEVICES--The U.S. Department of Energy in Washington, D.C. has jurisdiction over the sale of purported energy-saving devices, such as solar appliances. Call toll-free 800-424-9246.

FALSE ADVERTISING--Complaints should be made to the state Attorney General's Financial Fraud Division at 255-5763.

FOODS--For complaints about misbranded or contaminated foods, call the Food and Drug Administration at 261-3280. For problems with grocery-store sales practices, food advertising or sanitation, call the Retail Grocers Association of Arizona at 252-9761. For problems with short-weighted foods or foods kept on the shelves beyond their expiration dates, call the state Weights and Measures Division at 255-5211.

GASOLINE--To register complaints about the quality of gasoline or the accuracy of service station pumps, call the Weights and Measures Division at 255-5211. For suspected over-charging or price-gouging, call the U.S. Department of Energy, toll-free, 800-424-9246.

INSURANCE--The state Insurance Department, at 255-4783, investigates complaints against insurance com-

panies and agents, and can answer questions about
state laws governing insurance.

LAWYERS--Complaints about lawyers should be directed to the State Bar of Arizona, at 252-4804.

LEGAL AID--Community Legal Services, at 258-3434,
provides indigent persons with free legal assistance
in civil matters. To quality for the service, an individual must have an annual income of $3,925 or less.
A family of four must have an annual income of $7,750
or less.

The Lawyers Referral Service, at 263-0886, provides
a 30-minute consultation with a private lawyer for a
fee of $10. An additional half an hour costs $5. If
the client then wishes to retain the lawyer, further
fees are arranged according to the attorney's normal
rates.

Tel-Law, at 249-0773, is a phone-in library of 84
short tapes made by lawyers on general legal subjects.
The caller specifies the subject of interest and the
operator plays the tape over the phone. The service
includes 14 tapes in Spanish. It operates weekdays
from 9 a.m. to 7 p.m.

MOBILE HOMES & CAMPERS--The state Division of Mobile and Manufactured Housing Standards, at 255-4072,
regulates manufacturers, dealers and on-site install-
ers of mobile homes. The division also sets safety
standards for the installation of electrical and
butane appliances in recreational vehicles.

PEST CONTROL--The state Structural Pest Control
Board, at 255-3664, regulates residential pest and
weed control companies. The state Pesticide Control
Board, at 255-3578, regulates the agricultural use of
pesticides and herbicides and licenses the companies
that sell the chemicals.

REAL ESTATE--The state Real Estate Department, at
255-3585, handles complaints against real estate brokers, salesmen and subdivision developers. The department investigates suspected land frauds and mis-
reprentations about homes, commercial propery and land.

RENTED HOUSING—The Renters Advisory Service, at 264-7484, advises tennants and landlords on how to resolve disputes over deposits, rents, leases, eviction, delinquent payment, etc. The free service is sponsored by the Arizona Multi-Housing Association, a trade association of apartment owners.

For a free copy of the Arizona Landlord-Tenant Act, which outlines the legal rights and responsibilities of renters and landlords, call the office of the Secretary of State at 255-4285.

TIRES—Complaints about defective or unsafe tires should go to the National Highway Safety Administration in Washington, D.C., toll-free 800-424-9393. Problems with tire warranties are handled by the Los Angeles office of the Federal Trade Commision, 213-824-7575.

UNORDERED MERCHANDISE—The Federal Trade Commission in L.A. investigates companies that send customers unordered goods and then attempts to collect payment for the merchandise. L.A. 213-824-7575. If the merchandise or invoice is mailed, the Postal Service at 261-3417 can also investigate.

UTILITIES—Complaints about Arizona Public Service or Mountain Bell can go to the Arizona Corporation Commission at 255-4251. Complaints about the Salt River Project should go to that utility's Customer Information Center, at 267-9161. Complaints about SRP irrigation service are taken at 273-5275.

If you plan to excavate on your property and need to know the location of underground water, gas and electric lines, call the Blue State Institute, at 263-1100. This is a free service sponsored by the local utility companies.

WAGES—The U.S. Wage and Hour Division at 261-4223 enforces federal minimum wage, overtime and child-labor laws when the employer comes under the Fair Labor Standards Act (generally employers with a gross of $275,000 or more). If the complaint involves a smaller business, the state Labor Division at 255-4515 will investigate, but there is no state

minimum wage or overtime law governing these businesses.

WARRANTIES--If you feel a product warranty is not being honored, call the state Attorney General's Finan-
cial-Fraud Division at 255-5763, or the Federal Trade
Commission in L.A. 213-824-7575.*

COUNSELING

ARIZONA GUIDANCE CENTER--1745 W. Northern Ave.,
Phoenix, Az 85021. Tel 943-4629. The AGC provides counseling on personal problems of all kinds to all ages.
Fees are on a sliding scale, according to ability to
pay.

ASU COUNSELING TRAINING CENTER--ASU Campus, Payne
Hall, B-402, Tempe, Az 85281. Professional counseling
on marriage and family problems, death and other cri-
ses.

Counseling specifically for the elderly is available from several organizations: The Episcopal Church
Family Service, 253-4645; Family Services of Phoenix,
264-9891; Interfaith Counseling, 994-1329 (Scottsdale)
or 248-9247 (Phoenix); Jewish Family Service, 257-1904;
Tri-City Catholic Social Services (Mesa area), 834-
7777; Social Services of the Arizona Church of Latter
Day Saints, 955-8350; and the Salvation Army Senior
Citizens Center, 254-5187.

DEAF SERVICES

Special services for those with hearing problems
are available from: *Arizona Association of Deaf,* 311
N. Central Ave., Phoenix, tel 252-2294; the *Hearing
Education & Rehabilitation Society,* tel 253-2183; and
Samuel Gompers Memorial Rehabilitation Center, 7211
N. 7th St., Phoenix, tel 943-3484.

DENTAL REFERRAL SERVICE

For dental service references, call the Arizona

*Compiled by The Arizona Republic, and reprinted here
 with permission.*

State Dental Association, 3800 N. Central Ave., Phoenix, Az 85012, tel 264-3575.

EDUCATIONAL SERVICES

There are several sources of continuing education and training for senior citizens in Maricopa County. These include the Arizona Department of Security Training Program, tel 255-5036; the Jewish Community Center, tel 249-1832; Maricopa Community College, senior citizens program coordinator, tel 257-1413, ext. 221; Maricopa Technical College Consortium--Six Dimensions for People Over 60, tel 258-7251, ext. 228; and Scottsdale Community College, tel 947-5401.

EMPLOYMENT SERVICES

Senior Citizen Associates, founded in 1972 by retiree Douglas Addy, refers home-repair and improvement jobs to retired tradesmen who are on the SCA roster. Among the men who are available through SCA are retired electricians, plumbers, painters, locksmiths, tile-setters, masons and large appliance repairmen.

Anyone interested in utilizing the services of SCA or joining the enterprise to supplement their incomes, are invited to call (Phoenix) 275-1046.

One of the employment agencies in Maricopa that is operated exclusively for job seekers who are 55 years of age and older is called *Plus-60 Personnel Inc.* (The anomaly in the name of the agency, Plus-60 Personnel, and the fact that its services are available to anyone 55 or older is now just an economic measure. When the agency first was founded the purpose was to serve only those 60 and older, and changing it now would be costly.)

Plus-60 is financed by the United Fund and by contributions, and its services are free. The organization presently operates four offices: one at 1029 N. 1st Street in Phoenix, tel 258-7787, which is open from 9 a.m. to 4 p.m. weekdays; one at 5850 W. Northview in Glendale, tel 939-5698, open from 9 a.m. to 1 p.m. on weekdays; 7375 E. 2nd St., in Scottsdale, tel

994-2375; and 21 S. Hibbert, suite P-195, in Mesa, tel 835-0527.

Plus-60 places both men and women in part-time, seasonal and full-time employment. Categores of jobs and job seekers ranges from accountants to watchmen. A spokesperson for Plus-60 Personnel said there were usually more jobs than applicants.

Besides job placement, the agency conducts periodic classes and workshops in job-finding techniques and job orientation.

Other agencies with special interest in helping senior citizens obtain employment in the Valley of the Sun: Affirmative Action Program, tel 271-3711; Cooperative Employment and Training Agency (CETA), tel 262-6776; Arizona Department of Economic Security Employment Service, tel 274-4791; Equal Employment Opportunity Coordinator, tel 262-7716; and the Live-In Registry, tel 242-4815.

FINANCIAL SERVICES & INFORMATION

Planning and counseling agencies charged with helping senior citizens understand and organize their finances include: Family Debt Counselors, tel 258-5764; Assistance Payments, 252-7771; and the Social Security Administration, 263-1101, ext. 670.

FOOD STAMPS

The food stamps program is a program under which the Department of Agriculture sells food stamps to low income individuals and families at a special discount from the face value, or gives them free to families that are on welfare. The stamps are exchanged for food and other needed items at participating stores, thus increasing the user's purchasing power.

Many retirees with low incomes tend to confuse the the food stamp program with charity, and hesitate to take advantage of it. The stamps are not necessarily charity, since non-welfare households have to buy them. The main point is, by using the stamps you get a discount--which is no different from getting a discount for a packaged airline tour or a box of soap.

Eligibility for the program is determined by net monthly income and assets. To substantiate eligibility, an applicant must present such things as paycheck stubs, checking account and savings account books, rent or house payment receipts, etc., also any stocks, bonds, notes and so on.

After the application has been approved, the applicant will receive in the mail each month an *Authorization to Purchase* form from the food stamp office. This authorization specifies how many stamps the individual or family may buy for use during the coming month, and gives the cost. Payment in the form of a money order, along with the Authorization to Purchase, must be returned to the food stamp office by mail before the end of the month.

In Maricopa County (Phoenix, etc.) applications for the food stamp program may be made at any of a dozen offices listed in the white pages of the telephone book under Arizona State Government, Economic Security, Arizona Department of Food Stamps. The food stamp program information number in the Phoenix area is 258-9935. The state-wide toll-free number is 1-800-352-8401.

Eligible buyers who live in the Phoenix area may purchase the stamps over the counter at direct sales offices listed in the phone book under the heading given above.*

In Tucson, over-the-counter purchases may be made at 97 E. Congress and 5151 E. Broadway.

FOSTER GRANDPARENTS

If you would like to become a foster grandparent for a child with special needs, call the Alphamega Life Support Center, 1333 W. Camelback Rd., Phoenix, Az 85013, tel 277-5844. Day or night.

FOUNDATION FOR SENIOR ADULT LIVING INC

The *Foundation for Senior Adult Living*, an independent non-profit church-related organization, is rapidly emerging as a major mover in subsidy housing

Food stamps are now available through the mail.

for retirees in Arizona. The foundation was established to provide housing facilities, programs and services for all senior citizens in the four Arizona counties comprising the Catholic Diocese of Phoenix.

The foundation currently operates the Patterson
Terrace Retirements in Mesa, Desert Crest in Phoenix,
and smaller facilities in Avondale, Wickenburg, Williams and Lake Havasu City. Projects are underway to
open retirement housing complexes in Prescott, Kingman, Sun City and Phoenix. If a couple, one must be
at least 62 years old to qualify for residency in an
FSAL center, and there is an income limit.

For information about retirement housing now available, write or call the FSAL at 1825 W. Northern Ave.,
Phoenix, Az 85021. Tel 944-9641.

FRIENDLY VISITOR PROJECT

Sponsored by the federal government and the Phoenix YWCA, the *Friendly Visitor Project* trains people
to provide guidance, information and referral service
to senior citizens in the community, and to visit
lonely older citizens. The project also has a mini-
bus to provide transportation to those who need it.

Office for the project is in the YWCA Building,
230 E. Earll Dr., Phoenix, Az. Tel 264-3811, ext. 6.

Senior citizens interested in receiving visitors
for conversation and company may call the YWCA, the
Volunteer Bureau at 263-9736 or the Valley Christian Center, 258-5163.

HOME DELIVERED MEALS

There are several organizations around the Valley
that provide home delivered hot meals for people who
are unable to prepare their own meals. These include:

MOBILE ANGELS MEAL SERVICE (MAMS)--P.O. Box 32012,
Phoenix, Az 85064. Tel 279-7438. This program is operated out of several hospitals and retirement centers, and all the people involved are volunteer workers. Recipients must be referred by a physician,
the Visiting Nurse Service or a social service agency.

There is a nominal fee for the service, which is usually limited to four weeks.

NUTRITION PROGRAM--The Human Resources Department, Aging Services Division, 302 W. Washington, Phoenix, Az 85003, tel 262-7397, sponsors a nutrition program of home-delivered meals from several locations around the Valley. Call for qualifications and the address of the center nearest you.

COUNTY NUTRITION PROGRAM--The Maricopa County Community Services Department, Office on Aging, sponsors a nutrition program to deliver meals to eligible individuals in 16 communities outside of Phoenix. For the center nearest you, call the Office on Aging, at 262-3861.

PHOENIX JEWISH COMMUNITY CENTER--1718 W. Maryland, Phoenix, Az 85015. Tel 249-1832. Call for information.

MESA MEALS-ON-WHEELS--Community Services Bldg., 21 S. Hibbert. Tel 834-7777, ext. 427. Call for current details.

SCOTTSDALE MOBILE MEALS--Call for current details; tel 994-2323.

SUN CITY MEALS-ON-WHEELS--10632 Gulf Hills Dr., Sun City, Az 85351. Tel 974-9430. Call for current details.

TEMPE MEALS-ON-WHEELS--1500 S. Mill Ave., Tempe, Az 85281. Tel 968-9411, ext 287 or 968-4112.

HOUSE-SITTING

With household security against burglars, fires and other disasters becoming more and more of a concern, many people are reluctant to leave their homes vacant during vacations and business travel. This has increased the opportunities for retirees seeking part-time work as house-sitters.

In Tucson an organization called *Household Security Service* is doing a thriving business placing retirees as house-sitters. The idea, says HSS operator

Jane Poston, is to match the sitter with the requirements of the household--taking into consideration
such things as pets and plants that need special care.
    This is the kind of business that any responsible
older person can get into as a private entrepreneur,
with very little investment and very good prospects.

I.D. CARDS FOR NON-DRIVERS

The Arizona Department of Transportation, Motor Vehicle Division, 2339 N. 20th Ave., Phoenix, Az 85007,
tel 252-6661, provides free identification cards to
anyone over 65 who does not have a driver's license.
    Other DOT offices where the cards may be obtained:
Phoenix, 5225 N. 35th Ave., tel 261-7654
Scottsdale, 7002 E. 2nd St., tel 945-1823
Mesa, 43 E. First St., tel 964-7198

INFORMATION & REFERRAL SERVICES

The Community Council of Phoenix provides a cen-
tralized information and referral service for all residents in the Valley. Especially helpful to retirees, the service can provide some kind of help on
almost any subject that arises.
    The I&R Office is housed in the Community Council
Building at 1515 E. Osborn Rd., Phoenix, tel 263-
8856 or 263-8853.
    Other sources of information for senior citizens
include the following:

North Phoenix Information Center, 242-0005
South Phoenix Information Center, 252-5609
Citizens Assistance Phoenix Mayor's Office,
    tel 262-777
Glendale Citizen Participation Program, 931-5593
Scottsdale Citizens Assistance & Information,
    tel 994-2414
Tempe Citizens Information, 967-2001

IN-HOME SERVICES

Several organizations in the Valley provide various

in-house service for retired, disabled and ill senors. Among them:

APACHE JUNCTION

SENIOR HEALTH SERVICES--11015 E. Apache Trail, Apache Junction, tel 986-1681. SHS arranges visits to the homes of people who are 60 and over, isolated, in declining health, or with other problems. The SHS accepts referrals from postmen, mobile home park managers and other services.

PHOENIX

COMMUNITY HOME HEALTH CARE AGENCY--2601 E. Roosevelt, tel 974-2561. This agency provides intermittent skilled nursing, home health aid, medical and social therapy, nutrition counseling, etc.

HOSPICE OF THE VALLEY--214 E. Willeta St., tel 258-1572. Provides comfort and support to terminally ill patients and their families at home. A doctor's referral is required.

SUN CITY

SUNSHINE SERVICE--9980 Santa Fe Dr., tel 974-2561. Volunteers provide help to people suffering from loneliness, illness or bereavement. Various kinds of sickroom and health equipment are available.

LEGAL SERVICES

Anyone who requires the services of a lawyer and doesn't "have one" may make use of the *Lawyer's Referral Service*, tel 263-0886, or the *Legal Aid Society--Maricopa County Senior Citizens Legal Services*, tel 257-8524.

Other sources for legal assistance include the Maricopa County Bar Association, tel 277-2366, and the State Bar of Arizona, 252-4804. A pamphlet entitled *Legal & Protective Services for the Aging* is available free from the Community Council, 1515 E. Osborn Rd., Phoenix, Az 85014. Also see the Consumer Protection heading, and Tel-Law.

LIBRARIES

PHOENIX

The beautiful Phoenix Public Library at Central
Avenue & McDowell Road is especially popular with retirees. Besides its book sections, the library sponsors numerous special programs of interest to all
ages. Hours are 10 a.m. to 9 p.m. Monday thru Thursday, and from 10 a.m. to 6 p.m. on Friday and Saturday. Sunday hours are 2 p.m. to 6 p.m. except during
the months of June, July and August when it is closed
on this day. Main number of the library is 262-6451.

Branches of the Phoenix Public Library system include:

Acacia Branch, 750 E. Townley, tel 262-6223
Century Branch, 1750 E. Highland, tel 262-7411
Cholla Branch, 10050 Metro Parkway East, 262-4776
Harmon Branch, 411 W. Yavapai, 262-6362
Mesquite Branch, 3201 E. Bloomfield, 262-7298
Ocotillo Branch, 102 W. Southern Ave., 262-6694
Palo Verde Branch, 4402 N. 51st Ave., 262-6805
Saguaro Branch, 2808 N. 46th St., 262-6801
Yucca Branch, 5648 N. 15th Ave., 262-6787

The library also operates a Bookmobile Service.
For information about this, call 262-6560.

SCOTTSDALE

The Scottsdale Public Library is located in the im-
pressive Civic Plaza, at 3839 Civic Center Plaza, tel
994-2471. It is open from 10 a.m. to 9 p.m. Monday
thru Thursday, 10 a.m. to 5 p.m. on Friday and Saturday, and from 1 p.m. to 5 p.m. on Sundays from September thru May. There are two branches:

North Branch, 7301 E. Indian Bend Rd., 994-2374
Vista Branch, 7700 E. Roosevelt, 994-2329

TEMPE

Tempe's public library is at 3500 S. Rural Road.
Hours are 10 a.m. to 9 p.m. Monday thru Thursday,

from 10 a.m. to 5:30 p.m. Friday and Saturday and 2
p.m. to 6 p.m. on Sunday (from September thru May).

Bookmobile service provided by the Tempe Public
Library is available from 2 p.m. to 5:30 p.m. at different places around the city. For specific locations
and days, call 968-8231.

MESA

The Mesa Public Library, 59 East 1st St., is open
from 9:30 a.m. to 9 p.m. Monday thru Thursday; from
9:30 a.m. to 5:30 p.m. on Friday and Saturday, and
from 12:30 p.m. to 5:30 p.m. on Sundays. Tel 834-2207.

SUN CITY

The Sun City Public Library is at 16828 N. 99th
Avenue, tel 974-2569. It is open from 10 a.m. to 4
p.m. Monday thru Saturday. A branch is located at
10620 W. Peoria Ave., tel 933-7433. Hours at the branch are 10 a.m. to 4 p.m. Monday thru Friday.

SUN CITY WEST

The Sun City West Public Library is at 13801 Meek-
er Blvd., tel 584-2405. It is open from 10 a.m. to 4
pm. Tuesday thru Saturday, and is closed on Sundays
and Mondays

MEDICAL FACILITIES

Medical facilities in Phoenix include the usual
personal care, nursing homes and extended care facilities, along with federal and private hospitals and
clinics. Persons interested in nursing homes, personal and extended care services are cautioned to care-
fully investigate both the reputation and actual services of any facility before making any commitment.
As usual, there are some in the area whose quality
leaves a great deal to be desired.

Additional information on Health Care facilities
in Arizona can be obtained from the *Arizona Association of Health Care Facilities,* 6040 N. 7th Street,

Phoenix, Az 85012. Tel 263-9334.

NURSES, COMPANIONS, HOUSEKEEPERS

Retirees and others in the Valley of the Sun who are in need of nursing care, companions or housekeepers may obtain same, on an hourly, daily or live-in basis, from *Nurses for Home & Hospital Inc.,* 1502 W. Osborn Rd., Phoenix, Az 85015. Tel 266-6020. LPNs, nursing assistants and companion-housekeepers are available.

NURSING HOME OMBUDSMAN

Arizona's Department of Economic Security, Bureau of Aging, employs a special ombudsman (trouble shooter) to help people who have questions or problems relating to nursing homes. Call 271-4446 and ask for the Nursing Home Ombudsman.

NURSING SERVICE

Persons in need of home health services in Maricopa County may contact *Visiting Nurse Services Inc.,* 1515 E. Osborn Rd., Phoenix, tel 264-0721, for a visiting nurse. VNS is the certified Home Health Service Agency for Medicare patients in the county. It is supported by donations, United Fund agencies, bequests and fees. The office is open Monday thru Friday from 8 a.m. to 4:30 p.m.

Anyone wanting visiting nurse service may call the agency directly or ask the attending doctor to call. A nurse will respond to every call, but home service is continued only under the direction of a locally registered doctor of medicine, osteopathy or dentistry. The fee for a visiting nurse is based on the cost to the home health agency, and is arranged between the patient and the nurse.

OPERATION ID

Burglaries are the most common "public" crime in the Phoenix area, and Operation ID is a program con-

ducted by the Phoenix Police Department to help re-
duce the number of such crimes. The program consists
of home-owners borrowing an electric engraver from
any police or fire station, and marking items in
their homes that might be stolen with an identification number, such as their driver's license.

Persons who have marked their household goods and
valuables in this manner are given bright-colored
stickers to put in conspicuous places outside their
homes. Would-be burglars are usually turned away by
the stickers because they know any item stolen from
the home can easily be identified.

OPPORTUNITY FAIR

The *Senior Citizen's Opportunity Fair* is an event
held in the early months of the year at Mesa Community College and Glendale Community College. These
fairs give resident senior citizens as well as winter
visitors a chance to display handicrafts they have
made, and sell them at a profit. There is no charge
to exhibitors. The only restriction is that exhibitors be 50 years of age or older.

For details about the Opportunity Fair, contact
the Community Services Department of Maricopa County,
tel 262-3861.

REASSURANCE SERVICE

This is a telephone service, available to anyone
who lives alone, to help insure their safety and
health in case of illness or an accident that would
leave them helpless. The service is available seven
days a week anywhere within Maricopa County for a
very small monthly fee. To subscribe to the service
call 254-8328.

Other telephone reassurance programs in Maricopa
County include the Retired Senior Volunteer Program,
tel 944-4629; and the Retired Senior Volunteer Program of Tri-City (Mesa-Tempe-Scottsdale), tel 834-
6744. Also see Telephone Service for Shut-Ins
heading.

RUN FOR YOU LIFE

A Community Action program directed by the YMCA, the Governor's Council on Physical Fitness and the Phoenix Parks & Recreation Department, *Run for Your Life* is open to anyone up to the age of 60. Established community running locations include Monford Park, Papago Park, Harmon Park, Maryvale Park, the Downtown YMCA and Hermosa Park. For days, times and other possible running locations, call the YMCA at 253-6181.

SHOPPING ASSISTANCE

Retirees who are unable to do their own shopping may make use of the following services:

ASSISTANCE LEAGUE OF PHOENIX—7044 N. 7th St., Phoenix, tel 943-7463. The ALP provides grocery shopping as part of its home-maker service.

FOUNDATION FOR SENIOR ADULT LIVING—1825 W. Northern Ave., Phoenix, tel 242-7095. Provides grocery shopping for those unable to do so because of medical reasons.

SOCIAL SECURITY INFORMATION

The Social Security Administration in Arizona provides a toll-free telephone system for individuals seeking information about their social security. From Phoenix, Scottsdale, Tempe, Mesa and Chandler, the number to call is 263-1101.

In outlying communities of the Valley of the Sun (Apache Junction, Cave Creek, Deer Valley, Paradise Valley) dial zero and ask the operator for Enterprise 670, and you will be connected with the 263-1101 central number.

In other areas of the state, look in your local telephone directory under Social Security for the appropriate toll-free 800 number. When all the information extensions are busy, a recording in both English and Spanish will ask you to wait.

TELEPHONE REASSURANCE

ALPHAMEGA LIFE SUPPORT CENTER--1333 W. Camelback Rd., Phoenix, tel 277-5844. This organization makes social calls to shut-ins free of charge.

SUN CITY'S BOSWELL HOSPITAL--The Volunteer Office of Boswell's operates a telephone reassurance service for residents in the Sun City, Youngtown and Peoria area who are elderly and live alone or are incapacitated and need regular checking. For details about the service call 977-7211, ext. 376.

TEL-LAW

The Maricopa County Bar Association sponsors a information/counseling service by telephone that is of special interest to senior citizens and newcomers to Arizona. Called *Tel-Law,* the service is based on a library of tape recordings that cover such things as problems with lawyers, individual rights in numerous common circumstances, civil rights and responsibilities, senior citizen information, your home, consumer and credit information, bankruptcy, taxes, family law, you and your estate.

All you have to do to tap this extraordinary fund of legal information is to dial 249-0773, and give the operator the number of the tape you want to hear. Brochures that list all of the tapes may be obtained from the Community Services Bldg., 1515 E. Osborn Rd., in Phoenix, at senior and adult centers around the Valley, or by mail by calling 249-0773 and asking for the Tel-Law Tape Guide.

THE 62 PASS

Anyone 62 or over may obtain a pass from Maricopa County community colleges that entitles the owner to library privileges, free admittance to college athletic events, half-price registration in non-credit courses, and admittance to drama, fine arts, lectures and other cultural events at student rates--or free.

The numbers to call to obtain the passes are: Phoenix Community College, 264-2492; Scottsdale CC,

941-0999, ext. 210; Mesa Community College, 833-1261, ext. 380; Glendale CC, 934-2211 and Rio Salado CC, 258-4730.

TRANSPORTATION

Public transportation in Maricopa County is limited. Only a small fraction of the retired residents in the county live in areas that are even fairly well served by buses. Public bus service in the Valley is mostly on main thoroughfares. The route structure and service patterns are subject to frequent change, making access to many points in the city difficult or impossible.

As of this writing, there is no bus service of any kind on Sundays and holidays. Similar situations exist in other communities in Maricopa County—and in some it is worse.

A private car, or access to private transportation, is therefore an absolute necessity for most Valley residents, retired or not.

Route maps and schedules of the bus service that is available in Phoenix and surrounding areas—and it is gradually improving—can be obtained from bus drivers or at the Phoenix Transit Information Booth at 1st Street and Adams in downtown Phoenix, or by calling 257-8426. Senior citizens who are 65 and older may ride on city buses at reduced fares. Proof of eligibility is required if you do not look your age.*

TRANSPORTATION SERVICES

The following organizations provide limited transportation for paying and non-paying passengers:

AMERICAN CANCER SOCIETY—When no other resources are available, the ACS will provide rides to and from doctors' offices, clinics and hospitals. Tel 262-5861.

AMERICAN NAT'L RED CROSS—Provides transportation to medical, social and similar appointments in Phoenix and most surrounding communities. Arrangements must be made two weeks in advance. Tel 264-9481.

See p. 134 for important new information about bus service in the Phoenix area.

DIAL-A-RIDE NORTH PHOENIX--262-4501. DIAL-A-RIDE
SOUTH PHOENIX--262-4502. To qualify for this service, users must be 60 or over and have a special
identification card. For information about obtaining the card, call 262-7379.

DIAL-A-RIDE GLENDALE--931-5432. Call for details.

DIAL-A-RIDE MESA--962-1322. Call for partiuclars.

DIAL-A-RIDE PARADISE VALLEY--258-9977--This service is connected with the Paradise Valley Bus Company, and each honors the others transfers. There
is a nominal charge.

EASTER SEAL SOCIETY--252-6061. Provides transportation to medical and therapy facilities in Phoenix,
Sun City, Mesa and Tempe. Call for details.

HUMAN RESOURCES DEPT.--This government office provides bus transportation for shopping, from senior
centers and nutrition sites around the Valley. Call
for current locations and schedules. Tel 262-7379.

MARICOPA COUNTY COMMUNITY SERVICES DEPT.--Pro-
vides transportation to medical, social and recreational facilities for senior residents in county communities other than Phoenix, Scottsdale, Glendale
and Sun City.

VOLUNTEER ORGANIZATIONS

Most retirees quickly discover that helping others
is one of the prime satisfactions of life, and many
choose to help by working in worthwhile programs as
volunteers. Anyone interested in volunteer work is
invited to contact one of the following:

RETIRED SENIOR VOLUNTEER PROGRAM (Maricopa County
RSVP)--1825 W. Northern Ave., Phoenix, Az 85021. Tel
944-4629. Places volunteers over 60 in programs that
need help.

RETIRED VOLUNTEER PROGRAM (Tri-City)--1833 West
Southern Ave., Mesa, Az 85202. Tel 834-6744. Places
volunteers over 60 in non-profit organizations in

Mesa, Tempe, Chandler, Gilbert and Apache Junction.

VOLUNTEER BUREAU—1515 E. Osborn Rd., Phoenix, Az 85016, Tel 263-9736. Places volunteers in community facilities that need them/

U.S. ACTION PROGRAMS—522 N. Central Ave., Phoenix, Az 85004. Tel 261-4825. Provides volunteers for VISTA, Foster Grandparents, RSVP and the Peace Corps.

THE YMCA

The YMCA of Phoenix has numerous facilities and services of interest to senior citizens. These include residence rooms, swimming pools, gymnasiums, etc., plus regular programs of physical education, the arts and crafts, and social events. The main YMCA in Phoenix is at 350 N. 1st Street, and is open 24 hours daily. Tel 253-6181. Branches are:

NORTHEAST YMCA—2602 E. Clarendon, tel 955-3310.

NORTHWEST YMCA—5317 N. 17th Ave., tel 264-2209.

SOUTH MOUNTAIN—449 E. Southern, tel 276-4246.

WEST VALLEY—5260 W. Campbell, tel 247-2041.

The Scottsdale branch of the YMCA is at 3019 Civic Plaza, tel 945-6351. The Mesa branch is at 207 N. Mesa Drive, tel 969-8166; the Tempe branch is at 1801 Jen Tilly Lane, tel 968-9286.

All branches are open from 9 a.m. to 9 p.m. on weekdays and from 9 a.m. to noon on Saturdays.

THE YWCA

The *Young Women's Christian Association* is very active in sponsoring clubs and events of particular interest to retirees. Programs include classes of various kinds, educational and cultural events, as well as social affairs. Facilities at the main YWCA, which is at 230 E. Earll Dr., Phoenix, tel 264-3811, include a health club, swimming pool, tennis courts, massage and exercise equipment, meeting rooms, etc.

The YWCA has several branches around the Valley. They are:

GLENDALE BRANCH--8561 N. 61st Ave., tel 937-2707

SCOTTSDALE/TEMPE--4615 N. Granite Reef Rd., tel 949-7337

SOUTH MOUNTAIN--717 E. Southern Ave., 243-1775

Hours are 8:30 a.m. to 9 p.m. Monday thru Friday and 8:30 a.m. to 5 p.m. Saturdays.

NEW BUS SERVICE

Phoenix Transit has made significant improvements in its service. This includes several dozen new, wide air-conditioned buses, new routes and more rapid service on key routes. Monthly passes and ticket books also make substantial savings possible.

Bus schedules are now available from the Bus Terminal at 1st Street and Washington in downtown Phoenix, at Circle K Food Stores, Fry's Food Stores, Hospitals, most bank branches and the Municipal Building.

For information about routes and where to buy the monthly passes and ticket books, call 257-8426.

IV

RETIREMENT CENTERS
IN
SOUTHERN ARIZONA

Once known as the wildest frontier town in the
West, Tucson today is one of the most attractive and
civilized cities in the country. The historical tra-
ditions of the city have not disappeared, however.
On the contrary, they influence of its Indian, Spanish, Mexican and early American pioneer residents is
still very much in evidence in Tucson, giving the
city a special air that is both nostalgic and romantic.

Now Arizona's second largest city, Tucson was the
site of an Indian village as far back as 800 A.D.,
and probably thousands of years before that. The
Spanish arrived in the early 1500s, and were replac-
ed by Mexican authority in 1821. The American period
began in 1847, when the great area that is present-
day New Mexico, Arizona and California was ceded to
the U.S. by Mexico.

During the infamous Indian Wars of the 1860s and
1870s, Tucson was the principal city in Arizona,
serving as the state capital for several years. With
the end of the Indian uprisings and the arrival of
the railroad in Phoenix, Tucson became known primarily as the home of the University of Arizona, and as
a mecca for winter visitors.

Like most communities in Arizona, Tucson has been
growing rapidly since the 1940s, and is particularly
important to the state's economy, especially as a center for tourism and retirement. The *Pima Council on
Aging,* founded in 1968 to help develop and coordinate
services for senior citizens, is widely regarded as
one of the best programs of its type in the state.

Tucson sits in the broad Santa Cruz River Valley at an official elevation of 2,400 feet. The city is virtually surrounded by mountain ranges, the highest of which towers to over 9,000 feet and boasts the southernmost ski resort in the United States. Most of Tucson is situated on the eastern side of the Santa Cruz River bed, on a gradullly rising, uneven plain that ascends to the foothills of the beautiful Santa Catalina Mountains.

Despite its size and sophistication, Tucson still reflects a small town atmosphere that accounts for much of its special appeal to visitors and residents alike. The weather in Tucson, another major attraction, is even more benign than Phoenix. A glance at the following table shows why.

| | Average Temperature | | Rainfall | Rel. Humidity (%) | |
	Max.	Min.	(Inches)	A.M. 11:30	P.M. 5:30
January	63	67	0.75	42	38
February	68	40	0.93	37	30
March	72	43	0.57	30	26
April	82	50	0.43	23	19
May	90	58	0.19	17	13
June	99	66	0.14	16	13
July	99	74	1.93	32	29
August	97	72	2.22	38	34
September	95	68	1.36	32	28
October	84	57	0.75	31	28
November	74	44	0.52	30	29
December	66	39	0.84	40	39
Yearly Av.	82	54	10.63	31	27

For those who have allergies aggravated by pollen, the pollen count in Tucson is practically nil from late November to mid-February, and very low during the rest of the year.

RETIREMENT HOUSING

There is very little formal retirement housing in Tucson. As in Phoenix proper, the majority of the retired population in Tucson live in private homes and apartments, and in the ubiquitous mobile home parks. The best sources of information about private conventional housing in the Tucson area are the usual real estate agents and newspaper advertisements.

PUBLIC HOUSING

There are several public retirement housing facilities in Tucson for senior citizens with low incomes. These include the *Martin Luthern King Apartments, Craycroft Towers, Tucson House* and *Congress Garden Apartments*.

Because these public housing developments are subsidized by the federal government, applications must be submitted and prospective tennants must qualify for the income requirements. For more details and application forms, contact the Public Housing Office, 111 E. Pennington, Tucson, Az 85701.

RETIREMENT HOMES & APARTMENTS

BENSON RETIREMENT MOTEL--3314 E. Benson Highway, Tucson, Az 85706. Tel 294-1826. A residence motel for the retired, with maid service, linen and laundry service, three meals a day, a recreation room and heated pool, planned activities, transportation, personnel on duty 24-hours a day, and a night security system. Monthly rental fee.

CAMLU APARTMENTS--102 S. Sherwood Village Drive, Tucson, Az. Tel 298-9242. This was the first privately owned apartment complex strictly for the retired in Tucson. It has studio and one bedroom apartments, fully furnished, with maid service and all utilities. Other amenities include a laundry, beauty shop, recreation room and lounges with television.

Each of the Camlu apartments has an emergency inter-com system. Three meals a day are served, and there are many planned activities, including shoping tours around the city. There is usually a waiting list for occupancy.

CORONADO HEIGHTS APARTMENTS--3066 N. Balboa Dr.,

Tucson, Az 85705. Tel 624-1048. These apartments cater to both older adults and retirees. Furnished and
unfurnished apartments are available. Rent includes
utilities. Shopping and businesses are only one block
away.

ADULT & RETIREMENT MOBILE HOME COMMUNITIES

There are presently over 200 mobile home parks and
communities in and around Tucson, with new ones opening up regularly. Following is a list of some that
cater specifically to adults and retired seniors.

ACACIA GARDENS MOBILE HOME PARK—5505 N. Shannon
Rd., Tucson, Az 85705. Tel 887-1982. An elaborate
park with paved streets, street lights, security pat-
rols, a club house and pool with planned recreational
activities, Acacia also has individual mail delivery
and accepts reservations.

ADOBE CORRAL—2433 N. Castro, Tucson, Az 85705.
Tel 622-6870. A small park, with a recreation center,
and one block from shopping.

ALOHA MOBILE HOME PARK—810 W. Limberlost Dr.,
Tucson, Az 85705. Tel 887-9980. Adult and family sections; with a recreation hall and pool. Laundry.

ARTESIAN SPRINGS MOBILE HOME ESTATES—5445 N. Shannon Rd., Tucson, Az 85705. Tel 887-2581. Another big,
elaborate place with heated pool, club house, barbecue grills, shuffleboard courts, horseshoe pits and
ceramics club. Has off-street parking, natural gas
and laundry facilities.

BELAIR MOBILE HOME PARK—1455 W. Prince Rd., Tucson, Az 85705. Tel 887-4193. A small park with the
usual amenities. One block to shopping, medical,
church. No pets.

BERMUDA GARDENS MOBILE HOME PARK—826 W. Prince
Rd., Tucson, Az 85705. Tel 887-6991. All the usual
facilities, with planned recreational programs. Trailers for rent.

BLUE SKIES MOBILE HOME PARK—5510 N. Shannon Road,

Tucson, Az 85705. Tel 887-1171. Leisurely adult living in a large park with numerous recreational facilities; other amenities.

COVERED WAGON PARK--5757 E. Lee, Tucson, Az. Tel
326-2871. The usual facilities, plus furnished rentals. Near eastside shopping centers.

CACTUS GARDENS MOBILE RANCH--2333 W. Irvington Rd.,
Tucson, Az 85714. Tel 883-4771. Two miles south of
the city at 500-feet higher elevation, with spectacular view. Recreation center and swimming pool. Extra large lots; trailers for rent.

CAROUSEL RANCH MOBILE HOME PARK--1415 Wetmore Rd.,
Tucson, Az 85705. Tel 887-2050. Recreation hall and
swimming pool, with planned programs. Lots of grass
and shade trees; especially popular with retirees.

CATALINA VISTA MOBILE HOME PARK--3344 E. Kleindale
Rd., Tucson, Az 85716. Tel 325-2777. Recreation center, pool, shuffleboard courts. Large shade trees.

CRESCENT MANOR MOBILE HOME PARK--1150 W. Prince
Rd., Tucson, Az 85705. Tel 887-4452. Adjoins large
shopping center. Recreation center; laundry room.
Doctors, dentists, churches within walking distance.
No pets.

DESERT PUEBLO--1302 W. Ajo Way, Tucson, Az 85713.
Tel 889-9557. Family and adult sections. Spacious
lots. Club house with billiards, cards, arts, crafts,
dancing. Also therapy pool and saunas. Five minutes
to downtown; near shopping centers.

DOUBLE R RANCH MOBILE PARK--1635 West Roger Road,
Tucson, Az 85705. Tel 887-9938. Recreation center,
swimming pool and shuffleboard courts. Shade trees.

EL FRONTIER MOBILE HOME PARK--4233 Flowing Wells,
Tucson, Az 85715. Tel 887-0331. Prides itself on being "home" to senior citizens. Recreation center,
pool and shuffleboard courts.

FAR HORIZONS EAST MOBILE HOME ESTATES--7570 East
Speedway, Tucson, Az 85712. Tel 296-1112. Beautiful

view of the mountains; golf course only six blocks away. Near churches. Pool and recreation center.

FLOWING WELLS MOBILE GARDENS--4439 N. Romero Rd., Tucson, Az 85705. Tel 887-9871. Takes any size mobile home. Two-car off-street parking; pool, recreation center and planned activities. Laundry.

ROLLING MEADOWS--2121 S. Pantano Rd., Tucson, Az. Tel 298-8024. Prestige park with family and adult sections. Numerous recreational facilities. Paved driveways and cement patios.

FOOTHILLS MOBILE HOME PARK--1600 E. Roger Rd., Tucson, Az 85705. Tel 881-9101. Caters especially to retirees. Large shady lots, away from traffic noise. Usual amenities.

FRIENDLY VILLAGE ESTATES--1202 W. Miracle Mile, Tucson, Az 85705. Tel 888-5110. One of the nicest mobile home parks in Tucson, with large lots, swimming pool and recreation hall. No pets.

GREEN MEADOWS TRAILER PARK--1135 W. Prince Road, Tucson, Az 85705. Tel 887-4383. Large park with lots of shade. Recreation center and shuffleboard courts; plus the usual facilities.

THE HIGHLANDS--332 W. Matterhorn, Tucson 85718. Tel 297-2722. Off Oracle Road four minutes north of Casas Adobes Shopping Center. Sells or leases mobile home sites. Elevated desert setting, with good view of the mountains.

LABELLE TRAILER COURT--201 S. Norris Ave., Tucson 85705. Tel 622-1470. Prefers retired couples. Near shopping and bus lines.

LAMPLIGHTER MOBILE HOME PARK--3431 N. Flowing Wells Rd., Tucson 85705. Tel 888-3851. Near shopping center, medical facilities and bus line. Swimming pool and shuffleboard.

MONTE VISTA MOBILE HOME PARK--3702 N. 1st Avenue, Tucson 85719. Tel 887-5751. Close in near banks, etc. Paved streets; all the usual amenities. Golf nearby.

NOBLESSE OBLIGE MOBILE HOME ESTATES--3426 N. Romero Rd., Tucson 85705. Tel 887-9909. Comfortable living for adults. Numerous recreational facilities; planned activities. Sidewalks throughout; shaded spaces.

PARK WEST MOBILE HOME ESTATES--3003 W. Broadway, Tucson 85705. Tel 662-2589. Rated as one of the most beautiful adult mobile home parks in the country. Club house with numerous facilities; swimming pool, Jacuzzi bath, etc.

RANCHWOOD MOBILE PARK--5602 S. Palo Verde Ave., Tucson 85705. Tel 294-3822. Large lots; laundry room; pool, shuffleboard courts and other facilities.

RINCON COUNTRY--3411 S. Camino Seco, Tucson 85710. Tel 885-7851. Close to shopping centers. Club house and pool.

RIO VISTA MOBILE ESTATES--3201 E. Greenlee Rd., Tucson 85716. Tel 795-4598. Has separate adult and family sections, in an attractive northeast location with excellent view of the mountains. Heated pool; ramada; laundry.

SANTA CATALINA MOBILE HOME PARK--4445 N. Flowing Wells Rd., Tucson 85705. Tel 887-0836. Triple-wide trailers acceptable. Paved off-street parking for two cars. Club house, swimming pool and therapeutic bath. Laundry. Near shopping and churches.

ORACLE JUNCTION MOBILE HOME RANCH--Oracle Junction, Ctina, Miller Star Rt., 800 Tucson, Az 85737. Tel 825-3542. High in the foothills on the outskirts of Tucson, with hiking trails and spectacular views. Club house, etc., lots of trees.

DESERT WILLOWS--6001 S. Palo Verde Ave., Tucson 85706. Tel 889-9674. Billed as a "funtastic" mobile home park, the DW has more than most, including paved streets, lighting and perimeter security.

CAREFREE VILLAGE--4100 N. Romero Rd., (between Prince and Wetmore), Tucson, Az 85705. Tel 887-7811. Bus service at the entrance. Security guards. Plus club house, Jacuzzi and other recreational amenities.

SLEEPY HOLLOW RANCH--615 Alturas St., Tucson 85705.
Tel 624-7775. One of the most popular retirement parks
in Tucson. All the usual facilities, plus some.

SWAN LAKES ESTATES--4550 N. Flowing Wells Rd.,
Tucson 85705. Tel 887-9292. Has a private 4-acre lake
for boating and fishing; swimming pool; club house;
laundry; storage for boats and trailers; off-street
parking. One of Tucson's finest mobile home parks.

TERRA MOBILE HOME PARK--3833 N. Fairview Dr., Tucson. Tel 887-0591. In a quiet location but still convenient to shopping. Large pool, other facilities.

TUCSON ESTATES--5900 Western Way Circle, Tucson
(on the way to Old Tucson), 85713. Tel 883-2541.
Sites for sale in a country-club atmosphere. Has two
par 3 golf courses; large swimming pool and therapeutic bath; picnic area; shuffle board courts; arts and
crafts center; community kitchen; club house and
more.

WESTWARD HO MOBILE HOMES--3810 N. Romero Rd., Tucson 85706. Tel 887-0106. Billed as a "fun court with
country-club living at pioneer prices." Large color-
ed patios; heated pool; shuffleboard courts; weekly
potluck dinners; dancing, etc.

MOBILE HOME & RV NEWSPAPER

Retirees who live in mobile homes and/or recreational vehicles may want to subscribe to the *Tucson
Mobile Home News,* which is published weekly, or pick
up free copies at mobile home parks and other locations. For details, call 884-7120.

AGENCIES & SERVICES FOR SENIOR
CITIZENS IN TUCSON

PIMA COUNCIL ON AGING (PCOA)
The *Pima Council on Aging,* most important of the
Southern Arizona agencies concerned with the inter-
ests and problems of the aging and elderly, was

founded in 1968. The PCOA serves as an advocate, planner and coordinator of services and programs for senior citizens in Pima County. The Council is the focal point for organized efforts to prevent premature or inappropriate institutionalizing of older individuals, by helping to provide them with the will and the way to remain independent.

This help takes the form of home health, homemaker service, socialization, nutritional guidance and counseling. The PCOA also contracts with the Legal Aid Society of Pima County to provide legal services to the elderly. The Council also sponsors the publication of a monthly newspaper called *Never Too Late* for senior citizens in Tucson and Green Valley.

The newspaper carries information about changes in Social Security and other health and welfare provisions, plus activities of clubs and organizations in the area, and about things to do and places to go, pending legislation and other issues of interest to the retired and aged. Subscriptions to *Never Too Late* come with membership in the PCOA, which is virtually free.

The Pima Council on Aging is located in the Alameda Building, 100 E. Alameda, Suite 406, in downtown Tucson (85701). Tel (602) 624-4419.

ALCOHOLISM

Two agencies in Tucson are directly concerned with alcoholism: The *Alcoholism Council of Southern Arizona*, 2302 E. Speedway, tel 881-1011, which provides information and education on alcoholism; and *Alcoholics Anonymous* (mailing address: P.O. Box 5056, Tucson 85703), which has contacts available from 7 a.m. to 11 p.m. daily. For meeting locations and times, call 642-4183.

AMERICAN CANCER SOCIETY

The Southern Arizona District of the *American Cancer Society* (1735 E. Ft. Lowell Rd., Tucson, Az 85716) provides information and counseling for cancer patients and their families; arranges for trans-

portation to and from treatment, provides cancer
dressings, sickroom equipment, drugs for hardship
patients, and rehabilitation services for mastecto-
my, laryngectomy, etc. patients. These services are
free. Tel 795-5421.

ARIZONA LIONS EYE BANK

The Lions Eye Bank provides free examinations and
glasses for the needy, and also undertakes to provide eyes for corneal transplant, vitreous humor,
sclera and eye glands. The Bank, at 2719 N. Campbell
Ave., Tucson (85719) has someone on duty 24 hours a
day. Tel 327-7455.

ARTHRITIS FOUNDATION

The *Arthritis Foundation* operates two clinics for
treatment of arthritic patients, and provides therapy
at home and at the Tucson Medical Center pool. Patients must be referred by a Tucson physician, and
have lived in the area for a minimum of six months to
be eligible for treatment—which is free. The chapter
serves the six southern counties of Arizona. Office
of the Foundation is at 3833 E. 2nd St., Tucson (857-
16). Tel 326-2811. Hours are 9 a.m. to 5 p.m. weekdays.

ASSOCIATIONS FOR THE RETIRED

Tucson has numerous associations for the retired.
Since the meeting places often change with each incom-
ing president, contact the Pima Council on Aging at
624-4419 for current addresses and phone numbers. A-
mong the most active associations: American Association for Retired Persons; National Association of Retired Federal Employees; National Association of Retired & Veteran Railway Employees; National Retired
Teachers' Association; Service Corps of Retired Executives; and the Tucson Retired (military) Officers
Association.

Each issue of *Never Too Late* includes a comprehensive list of retiree clubs and associations.

BLIND SERVICES

TUCSON ASSOCIATION FOR THE BLIND--3767 E. Grant Rd. Tel 795-1331. Open from 9 a.m. to 5 p.m. weekdays. Provides social, educational and rehabilitation activities for the blind.

DIVISION OF REHABILITATION FOR THE VISUALLY IMPAIRED--A division of the Arizona State Department of Public Welfare, the DRVI operates regional eye clinics, a glaucoma clinic, and provides eye examinations, treatment, hospitalization, surgery and post operative care for visual conditions.

The agency also provides various vocational and adjustment services (crafts, talking books, bus passes, etc.), and sets up vending stands and snack bars for management by qualified blind persons. Many of these services are free. Fees for other services vary with circumstances. The DRVI is in Suite 414 of the Alameda Building, 100 E. Alameda, Tucson. Tel 882-5309. Call or write the agency office for more information and application procedures.

CONSUMER INFORMATION AND COMPLAINTS

BETTER BUSINESS BUREAU--100 E. Alameda, Suite 407. Open 8:30 a.m. to 4:30 p.m. weekdays. Handles inquiries and complaints about businesses and charities. For complaints call 622-7654; for inquiries call 622-7651.

DENTAL CARE

SOUTHERN ARIZONA DENTAL SOCIETY--For referrals and information about dental problems, call the society at 881-7237. Hours are 9 a.m. to noon and 1:30 p.m. to 5 p.m. Monday, Thursday and Friday, and from 9 a.m. to noon on Saturday.

ECONOMIC FUNERALS

The Tucson Memorial Society promotes preplanning of simple, economical funerals and provides informa-

tion about eye-banks, bone banks, cremation, etc. A
brochure is available. Fee for a lifetime membership, which covers all members of a family living at
one address, is very nominal. Call 323-1121 or write
P.O. Box 4566, Tucson, Az 85717 (Suite 401, 1011
Craycroft Rd.). Hours are 9 a.m. to 1 p.m. Monday,
Wednesday and Friday.

EMERGENCIES--911

For any kind of emergency in the Tucson area, dial
the *All Emergency Switchboard* at 911. This universal
911 number gives you a 24-hour operator who will connect you with whatever emergency service you need,
whether its the fire department, an ambulance, the rescue squad, a poison control center or where you can
get treatment for snake bite.
You may also get the Sheriff's Office by dialing
911.

DOCTOR OR MEDICAL REFERRAL SERVICE--If you do not
have a doctor and need a reference, call the Pima
County Medical Society at 327-6047. Hours are 9 a.m.
to 5 p.m. on weekdays. At night and on weekends call
327-7471.

EMPLOYMENT

Retiree Skills, 1517 W. Prince Rd., Tucson 85705,
is an agency set up to help men and women over 50 obtain part-time temporary employment. Anyone who suc-
ceeds in getting a job thru the agency pays a one-
time fee of $25 for setting up a file. There are no
other payments by the individual to the agency.
Part-time workers matched with jobs by Retiree
Skills are paid by the agency, which takes care of
all payroll deductions and pays workmen's and unem-
ployment compensation. For more information call Retiree Skills at 888-9396 or 888-8310.
The Tucson YWCA also offers a job-finding service
to senior citizens thru its Job Developer Program.
For details, call 884-7810, ext. 32.

FOOD STAMP PROGRAM

Senior citizens in Tucson who are eligible for the food stamp program (see the explanation in Chapter 4) and want to apply may do so between the hours of 9 a.m. and 3 p.m. at several locations around the city. For the office nearest you, call 792-8643 or 792-8577. If you are disabled, the food stamp program office will send someone out to take your application.

HEALTH AIDS

SOUTHERN ARIZONA MENTAL HEALTH CLINIC--1930 E. 6th St., Tucson. Tel 882-5241. Open from 8 to 5 on weekdays. Call for details about the various services available.

HOME HEALTH SERVICES

EASTER SEAL SOCIETY--920 N. Swan Rd. Tel 795-7542. Open from 8:30 to 4:30 weekdays. Lends donated medical equipment and appliances to needy patients.

PIMA COUNTY HEALTH DEPT.--151 W. Congress. Tel 792-8673. Provides professional nursing care and treatment on a visiting basis in the patient's home, under doctor's direction.

SICKROOM LOAN CHEST--1329 N. Swan. Tel 327-0981. Loans sickroom equipment to those unable to buy or rent it, on referral by a doctor, an accredited hospital or social agency. Open from 10 to 1 on Mondays, Tuesdays and Thursdays.

TUCSON VISITING NURSE ASSOC.--268 W. Adams St., tel 882-4150. Provides professional nursing care and treatment in the patient's home, under doctor's direction. Fees are based on the individual's ability to pay. Hours: 8 a.m. to 4:30 p.m. weekdays.

EXTENDED CARE FACILITIES

There is a large selection of nursing homes with extended care facilities in the Tucson area. For an up-to-date listing of the homes, contact the Pima Council on Aging, at 624-4419.

HOSPICE FOR TERMINALLY ILL

The *Hillhaven Hospice,* 5504 E. Pima Rd., tel 886-8263, provides care and treatment for terminally ill cancer patients that is "in between" hospital care and the limited care of nursing homes. Hillhave offers four phases or stages of care--home care; out-patient care; in-patient care, and a follow-up bereavement program. The work of the hospice is highly recommended.

HOT LUNCHES

The Tucson YWCA, 302 University Blvd., provides hot lunches for the aged and others Monday thru Friday from noon to 1 p.m. The cost for those who can afford to pay is nominal. The meals are free for anyone who cannot pay. Tel 884-7810.

INFORMATION & REFERRAL SERVICE
(HELP ON CALL!)

This is the primary source in Tucson for information, guidance and referral for individuals and agencies regarding community services. Special emphasis is given to the needs of the elderly and the handicapped. The I&R also provides a 24-hour crisis counseling and suicide prevention service by phone.

For local residents, dial 881-1794. Pima County residents outside of Tucson may call the I&R toll-free by dialing the operator and asking for Enterprise 881.

INVALID STICKERS

These are stickers, available from the Fire Prevention Division of Tucson, which are put on the front doors of the residences of invalids so proper steps can be taken to rescue them in the event of fire. Stickers are also attached to the bedroom windows where invalids normally sleep. The FPD maintains a record of the names and addresses where the stickers are placed, and keeps fire-truck dispatchers informed of their location.

JEWISH COMMUNITY CENTER

The *Jewish Community Center,* at 102 N. Plumer, tel 323-7167, has a special area for the exclusive use of senior citizens (Senior Now Generation Center), along with a trained staff that coordinates programs and activities for them. Other facilities at the center include a health club and swimming pool.

The center does such things as run hot-lunch programs for older adults several days a week, and provide free bus service to and from the center (for members). Non-members pay a nominal fare. Contact directly for information about current programs for seniors.

LA PIENDITA FOOD CO-OP

This food co-op, sponsored by the City of South Tucson, sells basic foods at 16 percent above cost to anyone who is 60 years of age or older. It is located at 420 E. 29th St. Tel 263-0656. Call before going, to make sure it is still in operation.

LAWYER REFERRAL SERVICE

This is a commercial service aimed at introducing competent lawyers to those unacquainted with local attorneys. There is a small fee for the first half hour of consultation, with subsequent fees to be a-greed upon. The LRS is at 201 N. Stone Ave., suite 218. Tel 623-4625.

LEGAL AID SOCIETY

The *Legal Aid Society* of the Pima County Bar Association handles civil matters for those unable to pay regular attorney fees. The Society does not handle criminal matters. Clients pay only court filing fees. 155 E. Alameda. Tel 623-9461.

LIBRARIES

TUCSON CENTRAL LIBRARY--200 S. 6th Ave. Tel 791-4393. Open weekdays from 10 to 9; Saturdays from 10 to 6 p.m. and Sundays from 1 p.m. to 5 p.m.

WOODS MEMORIAL BRANCH--3455 N. First Ave. Tel 791-4548. Call for hours.

HIMMEL PARK BRANCH--1035 N. Treat Ave. Tel 791-4397. Call for hours.

WILMOT BRANCH--530 N. Wilmot Rd. Tel 791-4627. Call for hours.

VALENCIA BRANCH--202 W. Valencia. Tel 791-4531.

COLUMBUS BRANCH--4350 E. 22nd St. Tel 791-4081.

EL PUEBLO BRANCH--101 W. Irvington Rd. Tel 791-4733.

EL RIO BRANCH--1390 W. Speedway. Tel 791-4468.

MISSION BRANCH--3770 S. Mission Rd. Tel 791-4811.

Senior citizens who are 65 and older and interested in areas of study not well-covered by the public libraries of Tucson may obtain guest library cards from the *University of Arizona* and use its ample facilities without charge.

MAILBOX MONITOR

This is a service under which postmen notify the Pima Council on Aging if letters pile up in an individual's mailbox, indicating that they might be ill or might have suffered an accident. The PCOA then alerts friends or relatives. Retirees may register for this service by calling the PCOA at 624-4419.

HOME DELIVERED MEALS

Mobile Meals of Tucson is a program for bringing two meals a day--one hot and one cold--to the handicapped and shut-in. The meals are prepared by the dietitians and kitchens of the Tucson Medical Center, the VA Hospital, Tucson General Hospital, St. Mary's and Carl Hayden Hospitals, and are de-

livered by volunteers. Recipients of mobile meals pay
according to their ability. The program is always in
need of volunteer help and additional funds. The office is in the Catholic Charities Building at 155 W.
Helen St. Dial 623-0344 and ask for Mobile Meals.

NON-DRIVER ID CARDS

If you do not drive but need an identification
card to cash checks, etc., you may obtain one from
the Motor Vehicle Division of the Department of Transportation at 635 E. 22nd Street or 2499 E. Ajo Way.
You need proof of identity (a birth certificate or
passport or several other pieces of identification--
or a family member who will vouch for you). There is
a small fee. For more details, call 882-5316.

OMBUDSMAN FOR THE ELDERLY

Tucson has a full-time professional ombudsman who
acts as an intermediary between senior citizens and
various public and private agencies and organizations
concerned with the interests of the elderly. The ombudsman helps senior citizens resolve problems and
complaints involving bureaucratic organizations. The
office of the Pima County ombudsman is in the Pima
Council on Aging office, suite 406, 100 E. Alameda,
Tucson. Tel 792-4131.

PIMA COLLEGE

A number of educational programs are available
for the elderly at Pima College. For details about
programs, visit or call the college, 2202 W. Ank-
lam Rd. Tel 884-6666. There is also a Senior Citizens
Education Center at 2700 E. Speedway. Tel 795-7013.

RETIRED PEOPLE'S DISCOUNTS

The *Retired People's Association of Arizona* has
arranged with many businesses around Tucson to extend courtesy discounts to retirees. Members of the
Association are provided with a list of the shops
and stores participating in this program. All re-

tired persons are eligible to join the RPAA (there is
a very small fee to cover printing and mailing a member ship card, but no monthly dues or other assess-
ments). Applications are available at senior centers
around the city.

VOLUNTEER PROGRAM

A nationwide volunteer program under ACTION designed to encourage and help retirees be "useful, needed
and appreciated," known as the Retired Senior Volunteer Program (RSVP), is administered by the Pima Council on Aging.

Volunteers, all 60 and over, do such things as
teach, tutor, counsel, work in public offices, sew,
tell stories, read, visit, etc. Two of the most popular volunteer groups in Tucson are a band of musici-
ans and a number of clowns--the latter strictly ama-
teur, but a hit in local hospitals, schools and nursing homes.

Anyone interested in becoming an RSVP volunteer
is invited to contact the program director at the
PCOA, 623-8677.

SENIOR CITIZEN CLUBS

For a current listing of dozens of Senior Citizen
clubs in Tucson, or information about particular category of club, including meeting places, dates and
activities, contact the Pima Council on Aging, 624-
4419, and request a copy of the monthly news bulletin *Never Too Late*, which carries a calendar of club
meetings and activities.

SENIOR CITIZEN CENTERS

ARMORY SENIOR CENTER--220 S. Fifth Ave. Tel 791-
4865. Open daily, with a variety of social, educational and recreational programs for senior citizens.
These include arts and crafts.

JEWISH COMMUNITY CENTER--102 N. Plumer. Tel 624-
8603. Numerous recreational, social and educational
programs.

VERDE MEADOWS CENTER—1360 E. Irvington Rd. Tel 791-4865. Open on weekdays, the Verde Meadows Center offers classes, games and a variety of social events.

YWCA Center—738 N. 5th Ave. Tel 884-7810, ext 36. Open from 9 a.m. to 2 p.m. Lunches are served, and there are numerous social, recreational, educational and sharing activities. Counseling and some transportation is available.

SCORE

This stands for Service Corps of Retired Executives and is a volunteer organization of retired businessmen who offer experienced counseling (free) to small businesses. The organization includes experts in numerous fields, and is always interested in more volunteers. Call 792-6616 or visit the office at 301 W. Congress, Suite 8-K.

SPEAKER'S BUREAU

Senior citizen groups, clubs or organizations interested in obtaining speakers for their meetings are invited to contact the *Speaker's Bureau,* which is administered by the Pima Council on Aging, tel 624-4419. The Bureau can arrange for speakers on a wide variety of topics of special interest to the elderly and retired.

TEL-MED TUCSON 886-5781

Tucson area residents who are concerned about their health or have health-related questions may take advantage of a special telephone medical information service operated by St. Joseph's Hospital. Callers have access to a pre-recorded tape casette library of more than 260 tapes on numerous health topics. The tapes vary in length from three to seven minutes.

It is first necessary to obtain a list or directory of the Tel-Med tapes, which are identified by numbers. For a copy of the directory, call the Tel-Med operator (886-5781) and give your name and address. Or you may get a copy of the directory from the

Public Relations Department of St. Joseph's Hospital, P.O. Box 12069, Tucson, Az 85732. Tel 296-3211, ext. 2000.

After you decide which of the tapes you want to hear, dial the Tel-Med operator at 886-5781 and give the appropriate number. When the tape is finished playing the telephone will disconnect automatically. If you want to hear another tape, re-dial the same number.

The program is not meant to be used as an emergency information service or to self-diagnose illnesses. Its purpose is to provide general health-care information and to help in the early recognition of symptoms of illness.

TRANSPORTATION

The Tucson Transit System provides bus service on the city's main thoroughfares at intervals of 15 to 30 minutes or more, depending on the route. Service is provided in the evenings and on Sundays on some routes. For a route map and bus schedule, call 882-9613, or contact the Tucson Transit System at 315 S. Plumer Avenue.

The Easter Seal Society of Tucson provides limited transportation for the elderly and others to various health services. The Society, at 920 N. Swan Rd., tel 795-7542, is open Monday thru Friday from 8:30 to 5. There is a charge for the transportation if the individual is able to pay.

TUCSON UNITED WAY

The *Tucson United Way* serves as a central coordinating agency for the activities of other agencies, organizations and individuals in the health and welfare fields. Goals of the TUW include promoting better health and recreational services through voluntary cooperative study, planning and action; preventing duplication of efforts and services and filling gaps in these services; and increasing public understanding of social services and the need for services based on high standards.

UNIVERSITY OF ARIZONA

One of the largest, most attractive and influential universities in the nation, the *University of Arizona*, in the heart of Tucson, has numerous facilities, exhibits and on-going programs of interest to senior citizens.

Information Desks are located in the main lobbies of the Student Union and Administration Buildings for the convenience of visitors. The desks provide visitors with various campus publications, brochures, calendars and other descriptive literature. The *Arizona Wild Cat*, the university's newspaper, carries a listing of all campus events, and may be picked up free at self-help campus newsstands.

Best thing for the senior citizen to do first is to go to the campus for a get-acquainted tour, picking up a copy of the U's *Visitor's Guide*, which provides historical background and general information about the school, as well as covering points of interest and a map of the campus.

VERDE MEADOWS RECREATION CENTER

One of the several recreation centers operated by the Parks and Recreation Department, *Verde Meadows* is at 1360 E. Irvington Rd., tel 791-4497. It has regular winter, spring and fall programs for senior citizens and adults. The programs differ according to the day of the week, and range from lessons in Spanish, pattern and ballroom dancing, current events discussions, hobby classes to card games and horseshoe pitching.

There are also numerous special events at the Center during the year. These include parties, fashion shows, dances and dinners. Many of these special events occur on holidays, such as Halloween, Thanksgiving Day, Christmas, Mother's Day and Father's Day. Visit the Center for a copy of its program of events for this year.

VOLUNTARY ACTION CENTER

An organization of vital importance to senior citi-

zens in Tucson, the *Voluntary Action Center* acts as
a coordinator between those who are willing and able
to offer their time and talent to hospitals and some
125 social service agencies in the area, placing
them with agencies that need help.

The Center serves the retired in Tucson in two
particular ways. A great deal of the service provided
by the volunteer office is directed toward the elderly who need one kind of help or another. And conver-
sely, the Center provides senior citizens with an
ideal opportunity to help those in need. Volunteer
work not only gives senior citizens something really
worthwhile to do, it also provides them with opportunities to make new friends and develop personal companionship.

The Voluntary Action Center does its best to place
volunteers in the type of activity they prefer—ranging from teacher's aids, secretaries, drivers, skilled tradesmen, visiting companions, guides, foster
grandparents, painters, to maintenance workers. As
one of the Center's volunteers stated recently, " I
want to unretire!" The Center is at 3833 E. 2nd St.,
Tucson, Az 85716. Tel 327-6208.

Green Valley

Another of Arizona's beautiful, nationally-known
retirement cities, *Green Valley* is 25 miles south of
Tucson (40 miles north of the Arizona-Mexican border)
in a particularly scenic section of the broad, slop-
ing Santa Cruz River divide. The eastern view from
Green Valley encompasses the towering ranges of the
Santa Rita Mountains. To the west are the copper-rich
Sierrita Mountains.

Officially founded in 1964, on part of what was
once a huge Spanish land grant that goes back to the
early 1700s, Green Valley is now one of the fastest
growing adult-retirement cities in the state. The
population is approaching 15,000 and there are presently several new subdivisions under construction.

Additional acreage in an adjoining pecan orchard offers vast possibilities for future expansion.

Most residents of Green Valley readily admit that they were first attracted to the community by its panoramic views from every location. The valley and the ring of mountains beyond present a truly magnificent vista that has changing moods as the sun rises and sets. It is always there; its fascination verging on the hypnotic.

Once captivated by the general area, visitors to Green Valley are next impressed by the beauty and serenity of the Spanish colonial and territorial architecture that prevails throughout the community--including the commercial areas. There is nothing else approaching it in the state. To preserve both this architectural beauty and the natural beauty of the valley, all utilities are underground.

LAY OF THE LAND

Green Valley slopes from west to east down to the Santa Cruz River bed. Elevation ranges from 3,030 feet at the southwestern boundary of the valley to 2,790 feet at the southeastern corner. In the southwest the terrain consists of low desert foothills divided by shallow arroyas that enhance the interest and beauty of the area--and serve as natural boundaries separating the community into neighborhoods.

One of the world's largest pecan orchards (over 320,000 trees on 5,000 acres) adjoins Green Valley on the southeast. (The nuts are processed at a plant at nearby Sahuarita.) There are also six world-famous copper mining operations (but no smelters!) in the hills just west of Green Valley. As part of their good neighbor policy, the mines offer tours of their facilities.

WEATHER

One of the healthiest environments in the U.S. Green Valley receives 86 percent of the possible sunshine every year, with an average of 220 absolutely cloud-free days. The weather in Green Valley is invigorating in both summer and winter. The average high temperature in July (the hottest month) is 101

degrees, and the average minimum in summer is 68 degrees. In January, the coldest month, the daily high
averages a bracing 67 degrees.

With the exception of a few days in July and August, the humidity in Green Valley is very low--below
20 percent during most of the summer, and averaging
40 percent the year around. The area also has a very
low pollen count, and is smog-free.

Green Valley has two brief rainy seasons--in late
December and early January, and in late July and
early August--during which there are some really
spectacular sunrises and sunsets due to cloud formations over the adjoining mountains. The average rain-
fall--16 inches--is enough to keep the natural desert
flora of the area green and blooming.

CHOICE OF HOMESITES

Residential homes in Green Valley include single
units, townhouses, rental apartments and mobile home
estates. Townhouses, like the homes, are sold on an
individual basis with the buyer having a guaranteed
title of ownership. Several floor plans are available
for the various home styles.

Conventional financing is available for home-build-
ing in Green Valley, with standard mortgages for up
to 25 years at prevailing interest rates. Buyers
range from couples on pensions to millionaires.

The rental apartment complex of Green Valley with
its shopping and recreational facilities, was conceived, financed and built under Section 231 of the National Housing Act as a retirement community for the
elderly. The privately built homes and townhouses in
the city are sold with covenants and restrictions
limiting them to senior citizens.

Green Valley has natural gas, its own water company, weekly garbage pickup, around-the-clock fire
protection and security, along with ambulance service.

MEDICAL SERVICES

Green Valley's own Santa Rita Health Care Center
includes a 100-bed nursing home, along with out-patient medical facilities. The Green Valley Medical
Clinic includes a cardiac clinic, an orthopedic clin-

ic, a dental clinic, a physical medicine and rehabilitation center, a radiology facility, a urological
clinic, a surgical clinic, plus physical therapy and
podiatric services.

The numerous hospitals, clinics and private spe-
cialists in Tucson are only 30 minutes away.

TRANSPORTATION

Green Valley residents who prefer not to drive
may take advantage of the Citizen's Auto Stage bus
service, which makes 10 trips daily between Tucson
and Nogales, stopping at the Green Valley Shopping
Mall both coming and going. The buses also stop anywhere along the route when passengers want to get on
or off.

SOCIAL & CULTURAL FACILITIES

In addition to several churches, social clubs,
arts and crafts centers, Green Valley also boasts a
huge Social Center that features a 700-seat auditorium used for the presentation of plays, concerts and
other activities.

The County Services Building, which houses the
Green Valley Library, is one of the largest structures in Arizona with both solar cooling and heating--
the first solar-powered major community building in
the state.

SHOPPING FACILITIES

Two of the most attractive and popular areas in
Green Valley are Green Valley Shopping Mall and Continental Shopping Plaza, which draw shoppers from
other nearby communities. Currently featuring over
100 shops and stores situated along covered walks
with ramps for wheelchairs, the two centers are the
largest shopping complexes in southern Arizona, outside of Tucson.

NEWSPAPERS & TELEVISION SERVICE

Green Valley has two newspapers, one weekly and
one bi-weekly. Early morning delivery service is a-
vailable for major Tucson and Phoenix dailies. Residents receive TV service from Tucson.

RECREATIONAL FACILITIES

The choice of recreational activities in Green Valley is wide. There are three 18-hole golf courses, including the private Country Club of Green Valley and the public Haven Golf Club, and one par-3 course. In addition to several recreation centers that offer numerous facilities for engaging in arts and crafts, there are also some dozen swimming pools, several tennis courts, a ballroom for dancing, and a riding stable.

CLUBS & ORGANIZATIONS

More than 70 percent of Green Valley's permanent population has professional backgrounds, and almost all the major social and civic organizations have active chapters in the community. There are also clubs for almost every interest.

NEARBY ATTRACTIONS

Several of Arizona's major sightseeing, cultural and recreational attractions are within a 30-minute to 2-hour drive from Green Valley. These include the famous San Xavier Mission on the Papago Indian Reservation just 16 miles to the north; Tubac, site of an Indian village for thousands of years, the first European settlement in Arizona, and now an Historic Landmark and center for artists, is 18 miles to the south.

Also, Tumacacori, a National Monument just south of Tubac; Nogales, Mexico only 45 minutes away, with its shops, restaurants, cantinas and bullfights; Tombstone, with its famous OK Corral, Boot Hill and other reminders of Arizona's colorful past; Colossal Cave, the world's largest dry cavern; Saguaro National Monument, immense forests of saguaro cacti; two famous canyon recreation areas, and more.

FRIENDS IN DEED

Friends in Deed is a volunteer group of Green Valley residents who provide transportation for the elderly and non-drivers in the community when they need to go to the doctor or shopping. The group also shops for those who are unable to do it themselves, prepares meals in emergencies, etc. Several telephone numbers of Friends in Deed are listed in the *Green Valley News* Classified Ad Section.

MOVING TO GREEN VALLEY

New and resale single family homes and townhouses in Green Valley are sold through Fairfield Green Valley Inc., P.O. Box 587, Green Valley, Az 85614 (231 W. Esperanza Blvd.), the primary developer. There are also a number of other real estate brokers and developers active in the area.

THE GREEN VALLEY VACATION PLAN

To give potential residents a taste of life in the community, Fairfield Green Valley Inc. offers visitors the opportunity to spend a week (or months) at its Vacation Center, which consists of nearly 200 townhouse style apartments in an attractive complex that includes a recreation center.

Weekly and monthly apartment rates at the Vacation Center are well below regular commercial rates. For information about the vacation plan, write Fairfield Green Valley at the above address or call (602) 625-2010.

Other Popular
Retirement Areas
In Southern Arizona

There are several other villages, towns and cities near Tucson and scattered around the southern and southwestern portions of the state that are also popular retirement areas. These are:

Arizona City

Ten Miles from Casa Grande, midway between Tucson and Phoenix in the strip optimistically labeled the "Golden Corridor" because of its future potential, master-planned *Arizona City* was founded in 1962 but real growth did not get underway until the early 1970s when it was acquired by the Fuqua Industries conglomerate. The combination residential/retirement commun-

ity consists of 3,500 acres of land divided into residential, recreational, commercial and industrial
segments.

The residential areas of Arizona City include homesites, single-family residences, apartment duplexes
and four-plexes. Lots in the community come in a variety of shapes and sizes, including large ones on a
golf course.

Arizona City recreation facilities include an 18-
hole golf course, a large swimming pool, tennis courts,
shuffleboard courts, volleyball court, cocktail lounge and a Community Center that has a library, lounge,
assembly hall and kitchen. The Harvey B. Adkins Memorial Park provides facilities for ball games, picnics
and barbecues. There is also a 48-acre lake, boasting
one of the Southwest's largest programmed fountains,
and a marina where rental boats are available. The
lake is stocked with warm water game fish. The Arizona
City Country Club contains a locker room, pro shop,
restaurant, bar and facilities for meetings, dances.

While planned as a conventional city, Arizona City
attracts a larger than average percentage of retirees,
and now has retired residents from about half the
states living there year-around. The community has a
permanent population approaching 1,500, but that figure swells to more than 2,000 during the "Snow Bird"
season.

For a community of its size, Arizona City has an
unusual blend of recreational and community facilities, all operated and managed by the Arizona City
Club, a non-profit volunteer homeowner's group. In
late 1979 Arizona City developer Michael Tennenbaum
turned over all the recreational and community facil-
ites, worth over $5 million in value, to the Arizona
City Club for one dollar.

Arizona City residents have their own bus which
transports them around the community and into nearby cities. Bicycles are also a popular means of transportation within the community.

For more information about Arizona City, contact
Arizona City Development Corp., P.O. Box 188, Arizona
City, Az 85223. Or call 258-0080 (from Phoenix); or
792-0658 from Tucson.

Oracle

In the Black Hills, sandwiched between the towering
Santa Catalina Mountains and Tortilla Mountains, some
30 miles northeast of Tucson, *Oracle* is another of
Arizona's little hill towns that will very likely become a major retirement center as the years go by.

At an altitude of 4,500 feet, which means cool comfortable summers and bracing but not frigid winters,
Oracle presently has a growing population of something
over 3,000--and most of the new people coming in are
retirees wanting to escape the heat of the lower deserts and the crowding of the large cities. The majority of Oracle's retired residents live in conventional homes, but the percentage that live in mobile homes
is increasing.

Oracle has a small library and a small attractive
park, so it is the cool, quiet life that is beckoning
retirees, not the physical amenities. Most residents
go into Tucson for medical care and shopping. To
reach from Tucson, take U.S. Highway 80/90 north to
Oracle Junction, and turn right. From the Phoenix area
go to Florence Junction via U.S. Highways 60/70 and
turn south to Oracle Junction.

Rio Rico

A planned community and resort 57 miles south of
Tucson and 12 miles north of Nogales and the Mexican
border, *Rio Rico* is a project of GAC Properties Inc.
of Arizona, and is taking shape on a 55,000-acre
tract in the rolling hills and valleys of beautiful
Santa Cruz County.

Situated at an elevation of 3,800 feet, the Rio
Rico site is bounded on the east by the Santa Rita
Mountains and on the west by the Tumacacori Mountains.
Rio Rico enjoys the same brilliant sunshine and low
humidity as Tucson, but it is a little cooler in
the summer and has enough additional rainfall to keep
the surrounding semi-desert greener.

Founded in 1969, Rio Rico presently consists of a

good-sized community made up of conventional homes,
apartments and townhouses, and the spectacular Rio
Rico Inn, which sits on a high ridge overlooking the
main portion of the valley. An adjoining Rio Rico
Industrial Park has several tenants with new ones
coming in regularly.

Rio Rico is again of special interest to retirees
because of its location and environment. Most of its
residents get acquainted with the area by spending
several days at Rio Rico Inn, which has complete resort hotel facilities, including tennis courts, swimming pool, golf course, skeet and trap range, riding
stables and campgrounds.

Land is being marketed in Rio Rico in several categories and five areas. The first of these areas is
called *Rio Rico,* and consists of 3,982 lots of at
least 10,000 square feet each, on 2,500 acres. Next
are *Rio Rico Estates* made up of sites measuring from
18,000 square feet to five acres and more. Third and
fourth are *Villas* and *Town Villas,* which are parcels
ranging from 10,000 square feet to three acres. The
fifth category, called *Rio Rico Ranchettes,* consists
of parcels from 18,000 square feet to more than 20
acres.

Sale of land in the Rio Rico development is handled by GAC Properties Inc., P.O. Box 1445, Nogales,
Arizona 85621. Tel (602) 281-8451.

Sierra Vista

In the southwest corner of Cochise County, just
above the Arizona/Mexican border, *Sierra Vista* is
the home of the U.S. Army's Ft. Huachuca, headquarters for the Strategic Communications Command, the
Electronic Proving Ground, the Army Intelligence Center School, and the Electronics Warfare School.

Ft. Huachuca was founded in 1887 as a cavalry outpost to protect ranchers and miners from marauding
Indians, eventually giving birth to the small Sierra
Vista community. In 1971, Sierra Vista turned around
and annexed the army post, more than tripling its
official population.

The economy as well as the social and cultural life of Sierra Vista continues to revolve around Ft. Huachuca, but the town and the nearby residential community of Huachuca City are gaining in importance as retirement centers, mostly for former military personnel who like the area well enough to continue living there after they leave the service.

Named from the spectacular views provided by the Huachuca Mountains and Sulpher Springs Valley, Sierra Vista is at an elevation of 4,600 feet, and enjoys an invigorating climate that includes about six inches of snow and 16½ inches of rain a year. Daytime winter temperatures are in the 40s and 50s, and summer highs are in the 80s and 90s. As in all of central and southern Arizona, the relative humidity is very low most of the year, and there is an abundance of bright, clear sunny days.

Sierra Vista is not as isolated as it might seem from a glance at a map. Tombstone is only 20 car minutes away; Nogales and several other border towns are less than an hour's drive. Tucson is only 70 miles away.

A number of land development projects are underway in the Sierra Vista vicinity, and indications are that the area will continue to grow as a retirement center, not only for ex-military personnel but for others as well. For more information, write: Chamber of Commerce, 1201 Fry Blvd., N.E., Sierra Vista, Az 85635.

Tubac

Now a tiny, picturesque community between Green Valley and Nogales, and a haven for artists and the retired, *Tubac* was the site of the first Spanish Presidio (walled community) in Arizona. It quickly developed into a thriving town, and was the starting point for the Spanish expedition that founded San Francisco. The first newspaper in Arizona was published in Tubac.

With the appearance of Tucson and the beginning of the Apache Indian wars, the settlement at Tubac began to decline and finally had to be abandoned. "Tucson,

Tumacacori, Tubac to Hell," was the way one newspaper
story described the dangers involved in getting from
Tucson to Tubac during the peak of the Indian wars.

The old Spanish Presidio and the area immediately
surrounding it are now a State Historical Park. The
little village, elevation 3,500 feet, is in an especially attractive portion of the Santa Cruz River
Valley, and will no doubt look better and better to
retirees in the future.

Toltec/Eloy

Also midway between Tucson and Phoenix in the so-
called "Golden Corridor," *Toltec* is a planned community begun on 13,000 acres in 1963, and annexed by the
city of Eloy in 1965. Residential areas in Toltec are
interspersed with parks and playgrounds, and there is
a Recreation Center. The architectural styles and exterior elevations throughout the community are varied
to enhance the beauty and charm of the dwellings.

Toltec/Eloy is in the northern reaches of the Santa Cruz River Valley, and like the Greater Tucson and
Phoenix areas is bathed in brilliant sunshine most of
the year. Annual rainfall averages about eight inches
and about the only time the weather seriously incon-
vencies anyone is when a dust storm blows up. This
usually happens on three or four times a year, and is
soon gone. Altitude in Toltec is 1,450 feet.

Homesites in Toltec are handled by Toltec Development Co., 3030 N. Central Ave., Suite 801, Phoenix,
Az 85012. Tel 264-0991.

Yuma

In the southwest corner of Arizona overlooking the
Colorado River (half way between Tucson/Phoenix and
San Diego) *Yuma* has long been a popular fall-winter-
and-spring haven for out-of-state retirees. Named after the original Indian inhabitants, Yuma had its
first European visitors as early as 1540 when Cap-
tain Hernando de Alarcon sailed his ship up the Gulf
of California and into the mouth of then great Colo-

rado River in an effort to link up with the Coronado
Expedition, which was seeking the Seven Golden Cities
of Cibola in the   northern portions of Arizona.
  Situated on a huge bend where the waters of the
wide Colorado narrowed considerably, Yuma served as a
major river crossing for Spanish, Mexican and then
American travelers going to and from California--
thus playing an important role in the settling of the
West.
  Yuma is officially recognized as the sunniest city
in the United States! The sun shines there 92 percent
of the time. Annual rainfall is 3.29 inches. Yuma is
also the warmest city in Arizona in the winter time.
The average daily high is 74.8 degrees in November,
67.9 in December, 70.3 in January, 69.7 in February,
77 in March and 85.8 in April. Yuma is 138 feet above
sea-level.
  Besides its eight parks, golf course, river and
lake fishing and boating, and other facilities available to senior citizens, the Yuma area also has a number of nationally known historical attractions, including the Yuma Territorial Prison and Fort Yuma.
The Mexican free port city of San Luis Rio Colorado
with its bullfights, night spots and shopping, is only 23 miles south of Yuma.

YUMA ADULT CENTER
  Most senior citizen activities in Yuma involve the
Yuma Adult Center, which offers a wide range of arts,
crafts, socialization and recreation for retirees who
reside in the Yuma area. A complete lapidary facility,
ceramic classes, pool room, card room and other facilities make the Center a hub of activity from 9 a.m.
to 4 p.m. Monday thru Friday. The Center is located
at 160 1st Street. Tel 782-5554.

CIVIC CENTER
  The Yuma Civic Center, at 1440 Desert Hills Drive,
tel 344-3800, offers similar programs for senior citizens and retirees in Yuma.

  The federally funded Senior Nutrition Program of
Yuma operates from the Adult Center, serving hot meals

and administering other community services such as
flu shots, for Yuma citizens 60 and over. A handicapped swim program is also operated by the Adult
Center, daily from 11 a.m. until noon.

ADULT/RETIREMENT MOBILE PARKS

Mobile home parks are popular with both winter
visitors and retired permanent residents in the Yuma
area. Some of the parks are communities within themselves, and range from modest to palatial. Some of
the better known ones:

CASA MANANA
2164 S. Camino Barranca
Yuma, Az 85364
Tel 783-7181

DEL VALLEE
1079 South Ave B
Yuma, Az 85364
Tel 783-8550

CHAPARRAL TRAILER PARK
1674 South Ave B
Yuma, Az 85364
Tel 783-7245

COUNTY CLUB MOBILE HOMES
150 W. Catalina Dr
Yuma, Az 85364
Tel 344-1300

DESERT ROYAL MOBILE PARK
661 East 32nd St
Yuma, Az 85364
Tel 726-0221

KENYON MOBILE HOME PARK
2402 West 16th St
Yuma, Az 85364

LAZY S TRAILER PARK
2100 West 3rd St
Yuma, Az 85364
Tel 783-8586

MESA TERRACE MOBILE ESTATES
3400 S. 4th Ave
Yuma, Az 85364
Tel 726-0499

HIDDEN COVE TRAILER PARK
2450 West Water
Yuma, Az 85364
Tel 783-3534

DESERT HOLIDAY MOBILE PARK
3601 South 4th Ave
Yuma, Az 85364
Tel 344-4680

DESERT PALMS MOBILE ESTATES
500 W. 28th St
Yuma, Az 85364
Tel 344-1016

TRAILS END MOBILE PARK
1075 S. Magnolia Ave
Yuma, Az 85364
Tel 783-9890

SHADY ACRES TRAILER PARK
1340 West 3rd St
Yuma, Az 85364

SHELTERING PALMS TRAILER
RANCH, 2545 W. 8th St
Yuma, Az 85364
Tel 782-2044

LOMA VISTA ESTATES
14582 S. Agate Way
Yuma, Az 85364
Tel 726-5798

WESTERN VILLAGE
3300 South 8th Ave
Yuma, Az 85364
Tel 726-1417

WESTERN TRAILER PARK
2002 West 8th St
Yuma, Az 85364
Tel 782-2044

SUBSIDIZED HOUSING
  Yuma's first subsidized housing complex, Catalina
Square Apartments, has 100 rental units. Its at 3200
South Catalina Dr., Yuma 85364. Contact directly for
more details.

OPERATION CAMPER
  Operation Camper is an educational program under
which senior citizens in Yuma may take courses of
their choice at *Arizona Western College* in Yuma. Anyone interested should contact the College directly,
tel 726-1000.

V

RETIREMENT COMMUNITIES
IN OTHER PARTS
OF ARIZONA

Bullhead City

On the Colorado River just below Davis Dam and due
west of Flagstaff and Kingman, *Bullhead City* ("Where
the Sun Spends the Winter") came into being during
the construction of Davis Dam in the late 1940s and
early 1950s. Because of the mild, sunny winters, the
panoramic desert-mountain scenery, and bountiful
fish and game in the area, many of those who worked
on the dam chose to live and later retire in the new
community.

Bullhead City has since continued to gain in popularity as a vacation resort/retirment area. The bust-
ling river town (the name comes from the shape of a
huge boulder in the river, later covered by Lake Mohave that rose behind the dam), is situated at an elevation of approximately 500 feet, in a scenic valley
that--as usual in Arizona--is bounded by spectacular
mountains.

The climate of Bullhead City is typical of the
Southwest: only three and a half inches of rainfall
a year; the lowest mean annual humidity in the U.S.;
an average wind of only four miles per hour; and
brilliant sunshine 90 percent of the time. Bullhead
City is hot in the summertime, but in winter it is
an average of 10 degrees warmer than Los Angeles.

Bullhead City is famous for its year-around fishing and river activities. Gambling casinos are located just across the river in the southern tip of
Nevada.

For details about housing, homesites, mobile home
parks and other facilities in Bullhead City, contact
the Chamber of Commerce, P.O. Box 66, Bullhead City,

Arizona 86430.

Gringo Pass

Gringo Pass (the official name is Lukeville) is the
gateway between south-central Arizona and Mexico, on
the route that leads to the Sea of Cortez or Gulf of
California, and *Puerto Penasco* (Rocky Point), which
is a popular fishing, swimming and vacation home resort in Mexico about an hour's drive from the U.S.
border.

Because of the proximity of "Gringo Pass" to the
Pacific Ocean,the fact that winters in the area are
especially warm and invigorating, and the presence of
the adjoining Organ Pipe Cactus National Park, many
trailer-livers spend their winters there.

The permanent community of Gringo Pass (or Lukevi-
le) is tiny. Facilities include trailer parks, a motel and laundromat, service stations, a restaurant
and cantina, general store, post office and curio
gift shop. For park rates and other information, write: Gay's Gringo Pass, Lukeville, Arizona 85341.

Lake Havasu City

One of the largest, most dynamic and colorful of
Arizona's planned cities, *Lake Havasu City* is another of the state's communities that was not intended
to be a retirement center but is nevertheless attracting many retirees because it offers so much in
the way of beauty, comfort, convenience, recreational,
cultural and commercial opportunities.

On a 16,630-acre desert slope overlooking beautiful Lake Havasu on the Colorado River, the city was
founded in 1963 by Robert P. McCulloch, president of
the McCulloch Oil Corporation conglomerate. McCulloch's grand concept of building an entirely new city
that would be "self-sufficient, beautiful and satisfying to those who want to work, live and play in
the surroundings of natural beauty" was keyed to moving his entire corporate complex from Los Angeles to

Lake Havasu and using it as a nucleus from which the
city would be built.

The project, one of the most ambitious ever attem-
pted by a private land developer, has been successful
beyond McCulloch's prophetic vision. One of the fastest growing cities in Arizona since its founding,
Lake Havasu City is expected to have a population of
some 60,000 by the end of the 1980s. *

In 1968 McCulloch bought the famous *London Bridge*
and over the following two years transferred it
stone-by-stone to Lake Havasu City. There he had it
refurbished and reassembled at a point where Lake Havasu Peninsula juts out into the lake. Then a channel
was cut across the peninsula, turning it into an island connected to the mainland by the bridge. While
this was going on the City of London built an *English
Village* on an acre of land next to the newly located
bridge, featuring a pub, restaurant, shops and other
facilities.

Already a tourist attraction before the multi-mil-
lion dollar international bridge transplant, Lake
Havasu and the London Bridge together are now one of
Arizona's major tourist meccas.

On the western border of Arizona, facing the Colorado River and California, Lake Havasu City is 490
feet above sea-level. The area averages only five inches of rain a year and relative humidity of 17 percent. The coldest winter temperatures are usually in
the 40s. The hottest summer temperatures (in July)
range from 105 to 108. The city has more sunshine
than either Phoenix or Tucson.

Besides its master-planned home, commercial and
industrial sites, Lake Havaus is a recreation lover's
paradise. In addition to golf courses, tennis courts
and numerous other land-based recreational and entertainment facilities, the 45-mile long lake in the immediate foreground is a total water resort--from
beaches and marinas to some fo the best fresh-water
fishing in the world. Just one of the colorful activities that take place on the lake is the annual
London Bridge Regatta, the world's largest inland
sailing series.

* *"Havasu" is Indian, meaning "Blue Water."*

The atmosphere and character of Lake Havasu is further ensured by the fact that it fills the only city-
sized area of land available for private development
in the vicinity of Lake Havasu. Both north and south
of the city on the Arizona side, the land is reserved
for Federal and State parks. Across the lake on the
California side, the land is either National Cooperative Land and Wildlife Management Areas, state parks
or Indian Reservations.

McCulloch's plans call for a balanced population
mix of one-third retirement, one-third service and
one-third industrial, and that is almost exactly what
Lake Havasu City has achieved so far.

The sales of homesites and commercial lots in Lake
Havasu is now handled by Pratt Properties Inc., 16838
E. Palisades Blvd., Fountain Hills, Az 85268. Tel
837-9660. Some 30 real estate agents in Lake Havasu
City handle both home and homesite sales.

Parker

This picturesque Arizona river town, 11 miles below Parker Dam (which forms Lake Havasu) on the Colorado River is headquarters for one of the larger,
more interesting concentrations of mobile home and
trailer parks in the state, and is favored by thousands of retirees who spend their winter months there
then move into northern Arizona, California and Oregon during the summer months.

Parker sits on the edge of the Colorado River on
state highways 72 and 95--which connect with U.S.
60/70 near Salome--and is 164 miles northwest of
Phoenix. The prime attraction is, of course, the
great Colorado River, which runs serene and blue-
deep in this area, with its year around fishing and
boating, and summertime swimming, tubing and water
skiing.

The riverfront, beginning at Parker and extending
north along the Arizona side of the river to Parker
Dam is known as the *Eleven Mile Strip*. It includes
mobile home parks and trailer courts, marinas, boat
landings, restaurants, shops catering to residents

and visitors, and the various other services usually
found in small towns.

   Among the annual events in Parker that draw additional thousands to the shores of the Colorado River
in the summer is the Nine-Hour Enduro, in which 100
speedboats participate in an exciting series of races that lasts all day, Altogether there are more
than 25 scheduled boat races in the Parker area in
the course of a year. Besides these special events,
Parker is noted as one of the Southwest's best fishing areas and as a gamebird hunter's haven.

   Even drier than the Valley of the Sun, with an
average rainfall of only 5.04 inches, Parker has a-
bout the same summer temperatures as the Phoenix,
Scottsdale area. But it gets a little cooler in the
winter. All things considered, it is bound to become
increasingly popular as a permanent retirement center.

PARKER MULTI-PURPOSE SENIOR CENTER--1217 Laguna Ave.
Tel 669-9586. Open from 10 a.m. to 10 p.m. weekdays,
the Parker Senior Center offers recreational opportunities, potluck meals and other activities.

RETIREMENT/VACATION HOMESITES
MOBILE HOME RESORTS

LAKE MOOVALYA KEYS
   Five and a half miles north of Parker on the riverfront, *Lake Moovalya Keys* is a retirement/vacation
home development that caters to boat-owners. All
homesites front on boat canals that circulate through
the community, and have direct access to the Colorado
River. The smallest sized home allowed on the deeded
lots is 1,100 square feet. All utilities are underground. A 24-hour guard allows only authorized persons
to enter the exclusive waterfront compound. The Keys
is managed by Robert Gory Realty, Rt. 2, Box 583,
Parker, Az 85344.

MOON RIDGE MARINA
   Another riverfront community, *Moon Ridge Marina*
offers both homesites and mobile home lots on the river's edge to vacationers and retirees. The marina

has underground utilities, all-weather roads, boat
docks and landing ramp. The area is restricted for
value protection. For more information contact Robert
Gory Realty, Rt. 2, Box 583, Parker, Az 85344.

BRANSON'S RESORT
   Eight miles north of Parker on the popular Eleven-
Mile-Strip, *Branson's Resort* has complete facilities
for year-around living; including a trailer court,
motel apartments, campgrounds, restaurants and grocery
store. Mailing address is Rt. 1, Box 710, Parker, Az
85344.

CASTLE ROCK SHORES
   A deluxe mobile home park three miles south of Parker Dam (eight miles north of Parker), *Castle Rock
Shores* has a special adult section for vacationers and
retirees. The park has a 2,380-foot shoreline, with
its own boat slips, a concrete launching ramp and an
enclosed marina. Other facilities include a large recreation hall and tiled restrooms. All utilities are
underground, and the streets in the park are paved and
lighted. Rt 1 Box 655, Riverside Dr., Parker, Az 85344.

RANCHO DEL RIO
   Rancho del Rio has both mobile home lots and motel
apartments. River frontage includes a beach, boat slips
and launching ramp. Mailing address is Rt. 1, Box 714,
Parker, Az 85344.

   For more information about Parker, contact the Chamber of Commerce at P.O. Box 627, Parker, Az 85344.

Payson

   An alpine town 85 miles north of Phoenix (about 75
miles from Scottsdale and closer still to Mesa), *Payson* is just below Arizona's famous *Mogollon Rim,* the
towering escarpment that separates the state's central
Plateau from the Highlands. Founded on the site of a
lumber mill, Payson quickly became popular for its
scenic beauty and cooler summer temperatures.
   Payson is now both a popular summer resort and home

for a growing number of retirees. Situated virtually
in the center of Arizona's fascinating wilderness a-
rea of tall pines, beautiful lakes and sparkling mountain streams, the town of Payson is permeated with the
tangy smell of pines and ozone, and has the type of
clear, cool air that makes a person happy to be alive.

Average rainfall in Payson is 21.8 iches a year.
The average snowfall is 25 inches. January temperatures
range from a low of 19.4 degrees to a high of 53.5 degrees. By April daytime temperatures are in the high
60s and 70s. Summertime highs are in the 80s and 90s.
The fall has warm days and cool nights, and is a rain-
bow of colors.

To reach Payson from the Greater Phoenix area drive
east on Shea Boulevard or McDowell Road to Beeline
Highway and turn north. For more information about the
area, contact the Chamber of Commerce, P.O. Drawer A,
Payson, Az 85541.

Jerome

Perched on a steep mountainside overlooking the
beautiful Verde River Valley, *Jerome* was once a thriving town, famous the world-over for its gold, silver
and copper mines. Then the mines played out, the population disappeared, and Jerome became a ghost town.
Years passed. The only thing that fanned a small spark
of life in the once colorful community were tourists
who stopped over to marvel at its precarious location
and empty buildings.

Then in the 1950s, the dozens of deserted homes and
commercial buildings, the superb view and the picture-
esqueness of the sleeping town began to attract artists who sooned formed a colony there. A few years
later the town was discovered by retirees and people
who like to refurbish old things. Indications are now
that Jerome will continue to grow as a combination
artist/retirement community. On Highway 89A between
Prescott and Sedona/Flagstaff, Jerome is just minutes
away from shopping and hospital facilities in Cottonwood.

Clarkdale

Also on Highway 89A, just south of beautiful Oak Creek Canyon and Sedona and at the foot of Mingus Mountains and Jerome, *Clarkdale* looks very much like a little town in Ohio or Michigan. Founded in 1914 near the site of a large mining smelter that processed gold and silver, Clarkdale now is a retirement center and popular tourist stopover between Oak Creek Canyon and Prescott.

On the banks of the Verde River at an elevation of 3,512 feet, Clarkdale has warm-to-hot summers and mild winters. Daytime temperatures in January, the coldest month, are usually in the 50s. Snowfall averages less than 2-inches a year.

The picturesque little community has a library, a community building and several churches. The nearest hospital is in Cottonwood, only two miles away. There is a golf course, swimming pool and park. The town is adjacent to two national forests, and is within minutes of several of the state's largest and most scenic recreational areas.

Besides the usual conventional housing and mobile homes, a number of residences once used by employees of the Clarkdale Smelter have been converted into retirement homes. For additional information, contact the Chamber of Commerce, Clarkdale, Az 86326.

Cottonwood

Nineteen miles south of Sedona and the mouth of Oak Creek Canyon, *Cottonwood* is near the geographic center of Arizona in the spectacular Verde River Valley. Founded on the banks of the Verde River in 1879 as a trading post for miners, farmers and ranchers in the area, the attractive little town is still a trading center for the Valley.

Hemmed in by high mountain chains and at an altitude of 3,300 feet, Cottonwood has a benign climate in both summer and winter, and is noted for its clear fresh air and attractive setting. These factors com-

bined have resulted in the small town becoming more and
more popular as a retirement community. At present, over 20 percent of the population is in the retired category. An additional reason for Cottonwood's growing
popularity among senior citizens is its Marcus J. Law-
rence Hospital, regarded as one of the finest diagnos-
tic and treatment centers in Northern Arizona.

Most of the people retiring in Cottonwood build
their own homes or live in mobile homes, but there are
some well-known retirement accommodations.

COPPER STRAND RESIDENT HOTEL
Designed for adult living, with room, board and maid
service, the Copper Strand Resident Hotel has private
and semi-private rooms, plus a dormitory. All rooms are
on the ground floor, air-conditioned in the summer and
steam-heated in the winter. All residents must be ambulatory, and may furnish their rooms anyway they wish.

Facilities at the Copper Strand include a lounge, a
private dining room, TV room, coffee bar and recreational area. The hotel is within walking distance of the
center of town. Mailing address is P.O. Box 1016, Cottonwood, Az 86326. Tel (602) 634-2520.

VERDE VALLEY MANOR
This is the first federally funded lease-rent rural
retirement center in Arizona. Located on 67.6 acres on
the outskirs of Cottonwood, and adjacent to Forest Service land, the center consists of efficiency, 1-bed-
room and 2-bedroom duplexes, plus a community building
housing meeting and recreational rooms and dining facilities. Address of the Manor is Verde Valley Manor,
Cottonwood, Az 86326.

For more information about Cottonwood, contact the
Chamber of Commerce, P.O. Box 412, Cottonwood, Az
86326.

Prescott

The first Territorial Capital of Arizona, *Prescott*
is now a small, attractive city that sets a mile high
midway between the desert and the highlands, in the

world's largest stand of Ponderosa pines. Long popular because of its beneficial effect on asthmatic conditions, Prescott is becoming increasingly important as a retirement area.

Summertime temperatures in Prescott are almost perfect. The average maximum afternoon temperature is 87 degrees, which in dry air is just pleasantly warm. When the sun goes down, so do the temperatures--falling to the mid or high 50s just before daybreak, at the lowest. Daytime winter temperatures in Prescott are in the invigorating 50s and 60s most of the time, and fall into the 30s and 40s only on the infrequent windy and cloudy days. Rainfall in the city averages about 18 inches a year, and occurs mostly in mid-winter and mid-summer. There is an average of 20 inches of snow in Prescott each year, but it disappears rapidly because of the brilliant sunshine that always follows. The city has 174 completely clear days, 99 partly clear days and only 92 cloudy days a year.

Most of the retired residents in Prescott live in conventional houses and apartments, which tend to be plentiful in the winter months and scarce in the summer, after the vacation and tourist season begins. The city has excellent hospital facilities. The Parks and Recreation Department sponsors a number of annual programs especially designed for senior citizens.

The Prescott Chamber of Commerce (Box 1147, Prescott, Az 86301) publishes a monthly guide to all the recreational, social, cultural and other public activities that take place in the city every year.

ARIZONA PIONEERS' HOME

Prescott's well-known *Arizona Pioneers' Home* is a state-sponsored nursing and sheltered care home with accommodations for up to 180 persons. Applicants for admission to the home must be at least 70 years old and must have lived in Arizona for a minimum of 35 years, including five years immediately prior to application.

The home provides lodging, meals, medical supervision, nursing care and other personal care as required. Fees are based on the individual's ability to pay. Ap-

plication forms are available from the Clerk of the
Superior Court in the individual's county of residence.
After being filled out, applications are forwarded
through the Superior Court to the Governor's Office.

HASSAYAMPA INN

This aged Prescott landmark was reopened in the mid-
1970s as a retirement hotel. A long-time showplace in
the city, the hotel cost $1.5 million to build in 1928
and today has an estimated replacement cost of several
million.

The hotel offers 70 single, double and twin-suite
accommodations. The apartments are leased furnished or
unfurnished, to suit the resident. Meals are available
daily and it is the option of the residents to choose
to eat in or out. There is also a restaurant and a
lounge in the lobby area of the hotel.

Several rooms of the Hassayampa are devoted to card-
playing, other games and hobbies. While there are no
medical services on the premises, the Prescott Rescue
Squad is only one block away and is on 24-hour call to
the hotel. For information about room vacancies and
rates, write Hassayampa Inn, 122 E. Gurley St., Prescott, Az 83601. Tel (602) 445-9454.

PRESCOTT COUNTRY CLUB PROPERTIES

A planned development on 1,600 acres of rolling land
14 miles southwest of Prescott, Prescott Country Club
Properties was inaugurated in 1968. Formerly the famous
Rafter Eleven Ranch, the development offers lots for
conventional housing as well as mobile homes. Community
facilities include an 18-hole golf course and a club
house. For more information contact Prescott Country
Club Properties Inc., Dewey Route, Prescott, Az 86301.

PRESCOTT GARDENS MOBILE HOME PARK--602 Copper Basin
Rd., Prescott, Az 86301. Tel (602) 445-9851. A large
and popular park, Prescott Gardens welcomes overnight
guests as well as permanent residents. Recreation hall
and shuffleboard courts.

PRESCOTT ADULT ACTIVITIES CENTER

Most interesting of the special senior citizen facilities in Prescott is the *Adult Activities Center*,

operated by the Parks and Recreation Department of
the city. Open from 10 a.m. to 4 p.m. Monday thru
Friday, the Center has a daily schedule of activities
varying from movies selected for senior citizens, to
dancing classes. The Center is in the Prescott Armory
on E. Gurley Street. Tel 445-8970.

YAVAPAI COLLEGE

Yavapai College in Prescott has a number of programs especially for senior citizens. These include
inviting resident retirees to host conferences; offering credit classes to senior citizens along with other
adults; offering hobby and avocational classes to senior citizens; hosting art shows, theatrical productions
and musical programs for adults of all ages; plus inviting adults in the area to attend athletic events
as spectators; making an enclosed swimming pool available for the exclusive use of senior citizens, and in
mixed classes; hiring numerous retirees to teach
classes at the college; giving retirees access to the
college library; and inviting senior citizens to attend
the schools Spectrum lecture series free of charge.

FRONTIER DAYS

The cowboy rodeo, which is unique to the American
West, was originated in Prescott on July 4th, 1888.
and remains today the biggest annual event in the city,
The festival is now called *Frontier Days,* and lasts
for three days over the 4th of July holidays. Besides
the traditional rodeo events, there are horse races,
parades, barbecues and more.

KELLER RETIREMENT COMMUNITY

Salome itself is little more than a roadrunner stop
on the highway between Wickenburg and Blythe, important
as a desert stop-over in years long gone. *Keller Retirement Community* is two miles south of Salome on the
edge of Harquahala Valley.

The developer of the site, Robert Gory Realty, P.O.
Box 583, Parker, Az 85344, offers homesites ranging

from one-hird of an acre to five acres--for people who
really desire secluded desert living. There is an on-
site recreation center. Basic shopping is available in
Salome.

Weather in the Salome area is much like it is in
Phoenix/Scottsdale/Mesa, with a little less rain and a
little more sunshine. Salome is some 100 miles northwest of Phoenix on U.S. Highways 60/70.

Sedona

One hundred and twenty-five miles north of Phoenix,
Sedona is the gateway to the southern entrance of Oak
Creek Canyon, widely regarded as the second most scenic
canyon in the American Southwest. The narrow part of
the canyon that most people identify with Oak Creek begins some 12 miles south of Flagstaff on Highway 89A,
descends a gradual 16 miles to Sedona, then spreads out
fan-like into a huge basin filled with great sculptures
of red rock.

Sedona and a wide sweep of Oak CreekValley/Basin to
the south are in this fabulous Red Rock Country. Some
of the gigantic rock formations, which tower up from
the canyon floor in solitary splendor, are flat-topped.
Others are shaped like Chinese pagodas, and still others
suggest other things. Among the more famous are Court-
house Rock, Cathedral Rock, Bell Rock and Coffee Pot
Rock.

Sedona began more or less as a summer resort and way-
station for the thousands who each year flock to the
recreational areas in Oak Creek Canyon. It also served
as headquarters for the many movie companies that film-
ed Westerns in the surrounding red rock country in the
1950s. Then in the 1960s, the picturesque village settlement took on an added role as a center for artists
and writers, and lastly began developing as a retirement center as well.

The big attractions in Sedona are the magnificent
scenery; the cool climate of the spring, summer and
fall months; the outdoor recreational activities available in the canyon and adjoining national forests;

seclusion from metropolitan life that is tempered by
the proximity of Flagstaff, Prescott and Phoenix, and
a certain ambience that is part of the wonder of nature.

Despite its altitude, the winter climate in Sedona
is surprisingly mild, considering that the high plateaus above the canyon walls are snow country where
very low temperatures are common-place. Because of the
protective walls of the canyon, however, Sedona basks
in warm sunlight during most of the winter. The snow
that survives the fall into the canyon is soon gone.

There are no retirement centers or communities as
such in Sedona, but there are many retired persons living in the area. Most of these have built their own
homes; some are renting. *The Village of Oak Creek,* a
planned community a few minutes from Sedona, attracts
a high percentage of retirees. Several mobile home
parks in the Sedona area are also popular with retirees, both during the sumer and winter.

SUNSET MOBILE HOME PARK

One of the largest of the mobile home facilities
is *Sunset Mobile Home Park,* a little west of Sedona on
Highway 89A. Sunset has separate adult and family areas
with single and double spaces for rent on a monthly
basis; plus a line of mobile homes for sale that are
set up free for purchasers.

Sunset Park is fenced, has paved streets with rolled curbs, ornamental street lighting and guest parking. A car wash, laundry room and storage areas for
boats, campers and travelers are among the facilities.
Recreational equipment and facilities include a large
club house, swimming pool, sauna baths for men and women, shuffleboard courts and card rooms. There is also
a community kitchen.

Parties, barbecues and potluck dinners are regular
events at Sunset Park. TV is available via cable. Several nearby country clubs offering golfing, and there
are a number of riding stables in the area.

There are dozens of cabins, summer homes and mobile
home/trailer park locations within Oak Creek Canyon
adjoining Sedona on the north. For more information

about the Sedona area, contact the Chamber of Commerce at Box 478, Sedona, Az 86336.

Switzerland-in-Arizona

This planned resort and retirement community is in mountain country near Payson, just below the almost sheer Mogollon Rim which marks the beginning of the Highlands. Many of the homes in *Switzerland in Arizona* are second-homes used in the summer season for weekends and vacations, but retirees from as many as 40 states have also been attracted to the community because of its invigorating climate, the tall pines and nearby trout-filled streams.

A Swiss motel, an inn, a theater, a restaurant built in the shape of a medieval castle and a community hall (with a huge clock tower) are among the facilities that help to distinguish Switzerland in Arizona.

The community is a project of Suburban Developers, Inc. Homesite sales are being handled by First National Land, 4240 Craftsman Court, Scottsdale, Az 85251. Tel (602) 945-4519. Residential lots for either chalet or mobile homes are available.

Wickenburg

One of the most picturesque of Arizona's towns, Wickenburg is some 54 miles northwest of Phoenix in the foothills of the Bradshaw Mountains—at a cooler than Phoenix altitude of 2,100 feet.

The town was founded on the banks of the Hassayampa River in the early 1860s by prospector Henry Wickenburg after he made a rich gold strike a short distance away. The story has it that Wickenburg picked up what he thought was an ordinary rock to throw at a stubborn mule. Attracted to the rock because of its extraordinary weight he discovered it was almost pure gold.

As the gold ore of Wickenburg's Vulture Mine began to play out, the little settlement gradually became a farming and ranching community, and was incorporated in 1909. In more recent decades, Wickenburg became known as the *Dude Ranch Capital of the World* after several of

the larger, more attractive working ranches in the
vicinity began accommodating winter guests from the
north and northeast. The town's gold mines and other
historical landmarks also made it a popular stop-
over for cross-country travelers.

In the 1950s and 60s, the combination of the excellent climate, the scenic Western setting and the
relaxed rural atmosphere of the town began to draw a
rather elite class of retirees to Wickenburg. Now,
over 25 percent of the population consists of retired senior citizens.

Wickenburg is quite a bit cooler than the Phoenix
area in the summer, and has slightly lower temperatures in winter. It has the same amount of sunshine
and none of the air pollution that comes with most
larger cities. In January, the coldest month, night-
time temperatures get down into the 20s and 30s,
then rise to the 60s on most days.

In July, the hottest month, the average low temperature is 69.1 and the average high is 102.4 degrees. Rainfall in Wickenburg is about 11 inches a
year, and there are usually one or two little snow
flurries in winter. The average per-year snowfall is
only 0.1 inches.

Most of the retirees who live in the Wickenburg
area have built their own homes or bought them.
Senior citizens who spend the winter there stay at
guest ranches, in motels or apartments, or in trailer parks along the banks of the Hassayampa ("Upside
Down") River, which runs underground in the center
of town but surfaces in pools several places down
stream. For more information about Wickenburg, write
to the Round-Up Club, c/o Chamber of Commerce, P.O.
Drawer CC, Wickenburg, Az 85358.

Yarnell

Some 16 miles northwest of Wickenburg, the Weaver
Mountains rise up from the desert floor, forming a
steep, almost mile-high wall that makes a spectacular
dividing line between the desert and the high plateau
country. The little town of *Yarnell* sits only a few

hundred yards back from the edge of this massive es-
carpment--78 miles northwest of Phoenix and 33 miles
south of Prescott.

Nestled in a tiny valley that is networked by ravines and pocked by huge house-size boulders, Yarnell
is another of the many picturesque communities in the
state that owes its founding to a prospector--Harrison
Yarnell, who discovered gold on one of its nearby
peaks in 1893.

Yarnell's population of 1,000-plus is made up almost
entirely of retirees who chose the location because it
provides real peace and quiet, has a very attractive
rural setting, is completely informal, cool in the summer and not too cold in the winter. It also has enough
rainfall that apple, peach and other fruit trees, along
with vegetable gardens, flourish with only a little
help from irrigation.

The residents of Yarnell live in private homes of
the conventional type, plus mobile homes on permanent
lots, secluded among the great boulders, in the narrow
ravines and on the slopes of the hills bordering the
little valley basins. There is a small business center
buttressing Highway 89 which passes through the eastern
edge of the community.

Yarnell has a community center, a park, and two well-
known tourist attractions: the Shrine of St. Joseph of
the Mountain, in a hollow a short distance from the
highway, and Carraro's Grotto, or the Zoo of Rocks,
nearby.

Winter temperatures in Yarnell range from a low of
22 degrees F. at night to a high of 69 in the daytime.
Summer temperatures go as high as 93 in mid-afternoon
and drop into the 60s and sometimes 50s at night. Snows
are infrequent in Yarnell, and are light and soon gone.

The community's drinking, household and gardening
water comes from deep wells that are so pure it does
not have to be chlorinated. For more information about
Yarnell contact the Chamber of Commerce, Yarnell, Az
85362.

VI

FACILITIES FOR RETIRED MILITARY PERSONNEL IN ARIZONA

RETIREMENT SERVICES PROGRAM

Arizona is especially popular as a retirement center among military personnel who are stationed in Arizona at the time of their retirement, as well as among those who have been stationed here some time in the past. This seems to be particularly true not only because they find the climate and other environmental factors attractive, but also because they find more opportunities here for beginning new careers in business, finance, education and politics.

There are a total of 11 Air Force, Army and Marine installations in Arizona that have various facilities available to retired military personnel and their dependents. These installations include Luke Air Force Base west of Phoenix; Williams Air Force Base in Chandler; Gila Bend Air Force Base in Gila Bend; Davis-Monthan Air Force Base in Tucson; the Marine Corps Air Station in Yuma; the Yuma Proving Ground; Ft. Huachuca in Sierra Vista about one hour south of Tucson; VA hospitals in Phoenix, Tucson and Prescott, and the USA Advisory Group in Phoenix.

The Air Force has the largest number of facilities in Arizona, but the Army appears to have more of an organized system designed specifically to serve its retired personnel. The Army's system is called the Retired Services Program, and includes Retirement Services Offices in all Army districts. These offices provide advice and guidance on nearly any subject relating to life after retirement.

Another key service of the Retirement Services Office is the operation of libraries containing publi-

cations of special interest to military personnel
with 18 more years of active service. These publications include *Who's Hiring Who, Employment Newsletter,
Scholarships and Financial Aids, Retiree's Benefit
Checklist* and many more. Retired Army personnel are
encouraged to visit or call their nearest Retirement
Services Office.

The Retirement Services Office in Arizona is at
Headquarters, Ft. Huachuca, ATTN: CCH-PCA-AT, Fort
Huachuca, Arizona 85613. The office is in Building
22408. Hours of operation are 7:30 a.m. to 4:15. p.m.
Monday thru Friday except on holidays. Tel 538-3610
or 5733.

Headquarters Ft. Huachuca sponsors an annual Retired Activities Day (Open House) on Saturday prece-
ding Columbus Day in October. All military retirees,
widows/widowers and their families are invited to attend. The aim of the occasion is to make sure retired
personnel are aware of all the services available to
them, and to provide on-the-spot guidance and counseling in booths set up for that purpose. The day is
also marked by social and festive events.

The four largest military establishments in Arizo-
na--and those that contribute the largest number of
retirees to the state--have the largest array of facilities and services of interest to the retired military. These four are Luke Air Force Base, Williams
Air Force Base, Davis-Monthan Air Force Base, and
Ft. Huachuca.

LUKE AIR FORCE BASE

Luke Air Force Base is situated at the western
end of the Valley of the Sun, about 40 miles from
Phoenix, and only a short distance from the base of
the White Tank Mountains. Mailing address for matters
relating to retirement is: Personal Affairs Officer,
DPMS, Luke Air Force Base, 85309, Arizona. Tel 935-
7851.

Luke AFB is the home of the Tactical Air Command's
58th Tactical Fighter Training Wing, the largest in
the U.S., and also serves as a center for training

German Air Force and Navy pilots. The base has numerous facilities and services available to retired military personnel

BASE EXCHANGE--Luke's Base Exchange main store carries a large selection of consumer merchandise, and has 15 other food and service activities, including a Customer Service Department where special orders may be placed.

COMMISSARY--The Commissary at Luke offers a full selection of fresh meats and produce, dairy products, frozen and canned foods and various household items. A Commissary Annex is located just north of Thunderbird Road as you enter the housing area from the base. It is mandatory that those using the Commissary facilities show proper identification before they are allowed in. The Commissary is open to retired military personnel and their authorized dependents or agents.

HOSPITAL--The Luke AFB hospital is a multi-million dollar facility with the latest equipment, but there are some medical services that may not be provided for retirees and their dependents because of a shortage of doctors. If this is the case, retirees and their families are authorized to go to civilian doctors under a deductable-fee plan. For details call the hospital's Registrar's Office.

LUKE FEDERAL CREDIT UNION--Retired military personnel who live in the Phoenix area are eligible for membership in the Luke Federal Credit Union. The union has several million dollars in assets and a comparable sum loaned out to its members.

PERSONAL AFFAIRS OFFICE--This is the key office at Luke AFB for retired personnel. Its services include preparing emergency data cards, ID cards, and helping in such matters as insurance, credit unions, survivors benefits, estate planning, veterans benefits, etc.

RECREATION FACILITIES--Among the recreational facilities at Luke are a golf-driving range and pro shop, an arts and crafts center, an auto hobby shop, a photographic work shop and an Aero Club. For more information call 937-0079.

GYMNASIUM--This is another of Luke's many facilities that retired military personnel may utilize. It has basketball courts, a combination handball and squash court, weight-lifting equipment, a massage room and steam room; and adjoining facilities include three swimming pools, tennis courts, two baseball fields and a football field.

LIBRARY--Luke's library is open seven days a week. In addition to some 20,000 books, it has subscriptions to over 200 leading magazines and newspapers, a listening room and several hundred tapes and recordings.

FT. TUTHILL--Luke also has its own mountain resort located near Flagstaff just off of the Black Canyon Freeway. Facilities there include a lodge, wooden huts, trailers and campsites for tents and mobile homes. Showers and restrooms are centrally located. For reservations, which are a must, call Luke's Silver Wings Community Center.

WILLIAMS AIR FORCE BASE

On the eastern outskirts of Chandler, and only a few minutes southeast of Phoenix via I-10 Freeway, Williams Air Force Base is home for the U.S. Air Force's 3525th Air Base Group. A relatively small base, Williams looks more like a country club than the traditional military installation. It has the usual base facilities and services.

U.S. AIRFORCE RETIREMENT PROGRAM INFORMATION CENTER--The Retired Affairs Office at Williams is located in Building 85, opposite the Guard Gate at the main entrance of the base. The office is open Tuesday thru Friday from 9 a.m. to 3 p.m. To call, dial the main Williams AFB switchboard at 988-2661. The office acts as an information and counseling center for all retired military personnel and their dependents.

WAFB HOSPITAL--In Building S, just inside the main gate between E and G Streets, the Williams Hospital provides short-term general medical, surgical and dental care. For information and appointments call

988-6814 or 2668. Retired personnel may receive imm-
unizations on Monday and Wednesday afternoons by ap-
pointment only.

COMMISSARY--The Williams Commissary is in Building
S-400. Call for current hours.

CREDIT UNION--The WAFB Credit Union has four offices: in Mesa at 325 N. Stapley Dr., tel 833-4533;
the Papago Branch in Phoenix at 1852 N. 52nd St., Tel
275-1914; the Air National Guard Branch, tel 273-0192
and the base branch in Building S-683, tel 988-1591.

OFFICER'S CLUB--A large, attractive facility with
over 1,000 members, the Williams Officer's Club has
a main dining room and bar, stag bar, and informal
dining room, ballroom, and banquet room for special
occasions, and its own swimming pool. Activities include floorshows on weekends. Building S-300.

NCO CLUB--Also a large, popular facility, the NCO
Club at Williams is in Building S-370.

GOLF COURSE--Williams has a 9-hole golf course
with pro shop and snack bar, just north of the main
gate. The course is open Tuesday thru Sunday from 7
a.m. to 6 p.m.

WAFB LIBRARY--In Building S-11, the library has
over 23,000 books, plus subscriptions to over 100
publications and four large newspapers. Hours are
from 10 a.m. to 8 p.m. weekdays and from 1 p.m. to
6 p.m. on weekends.

BOATING & FISHING--The Air Force maintains its
own boating and fishing facility at Arizona's famous
Apache Lake, 53 miles north of the base on the Salt
River. The resort complex, called *Waterdog,* has a
small fleet of rental fishing boats and over a dozen
six-person cabin cruisers equipped with refrigerators,
butane stoves and space heaters. Waterdog is open
every day all year-around.

For reservations at the Air Force lake facility,
call Personnel Services at 988-2592 (Building S-13).
All kinds of camping equipment is available from
Special Services in the same building. For information about other recreational opportunities at WAFB--

bowling, hobby shops, movies, swimming, gym activit-
ies--call Special Services at 988-6636.

DAVIS-MONTHAN AIR FORCE BASE

Adjoining the city of Tucson on the southeast,
Davis-Monthan Air Force Base (often referred to as
DM), is a large, diversified military community that
is an attractive city within itself. The home of the
390th Strategic Missile Wing and the 100th Reconnai-
ssance Wing (SAC's only U-2 unit), DM has all the
services and facilities necessary to make its residents virtually self-sufficient. Among the bases services that are of interest to retired military:

USAF REGIONAL HOSPITAL--In addition to providing
general hospital care for active duty and retired military familes in the Tucson area, DM's large Regional
Hospital also serves as a specialty care referral
center for Luke and Williams Air Force Bases near
Phoenix. The fully equipped hospital is on P Street,
one-half mile east of Vandenberg Village. For details
call 748-3113.

COMMISSARY--The DM Commissary is at Third and I
Streets across from Building S-1. Call for current
operating hours.

BASE EXCHANGE--The main DM Base Exchange is in
Building 1430 at Second and E Streets. Call for current operating hours.

PERSONAL AFFAIRS OFFICE--This is the office concerned with maters of interest to retired military
personnel. The staff provides assistance on government insurance, commercial insurance, voting information, state bonuses, overseas counseling, survivor's
benefits, medical care, social security, the G.I.
Bill, Air Force Aid and estate planning. The office
is in Building 1003.

CREDIT UNION--The DM Federal Credit Union main office is at 2222 S. Crayfroft Rd., in Tucson. An on-
base branch is located at Third and F Streets.

LIBRARY--In Building 3210 on the corner of Craycroft Road and I Street, the large and popular DM
library has a wide selection of books, magazines,

newspapers from local and large cities around the country, records and tapes.

OFFICER'S CLUB--The DM Officer's Open Mess, at Craycroft and 10th Street, is regarded as one of the finest officer's clubs in the Air Force. Besides the main dining room there is a main bar and a poly bar, plus a package store. The club presents a variety of entertainment regularly, including lounge acts, membership parties, night gourmet specialties, and Sunday champagne brunches.

NCO CLUB--The NCO Open Mess offers a variety of facilities to its members, including a dining room, banquet rooms, bar lounges and swimming pool. The club features name bands every Friday and Saturday night, with special buffets and other events during the year.

LEISURE-TIME FACILITIES

AERO CLUB--Located in Building U-4806 on the flight-line, DM's Aero Club offers both flight-training and recreational flying. Business meetings are held in the Community Center (Bldg. 4455) on the second Tuesday each month. Prospective members are invited to attend.

BOWLING ALLEY--One of the largest and most modern Air Force bowling alleys, the center has lockers for personal bowling equipment, a bowling supply shop, and snackbar. The lanes are open Monday thru Saturday from 10 a.m. to midnight, and on Sunday from noon to midnight.

GOLF COURSE--DM has its own 18-hole golf course, with electric carts available for rent. There is also a putting green, driving range and chipping area. The club house includes a pro shop and snackbar.

GYMNASIUM--The DM gym has body-building, reducing and conditioning equipment, two handball courts; basketball, volleyball and badminton courts; a sauna bath; dressing and shower rooms, locker and towel service. Seating capacity of the gym, used for varsity games and special functions, is 800. It is reserved for women from 9 a.m. to 11 a.m. Tuesdays and Thursdays.

ROD & GUN CLUB--Members of the Rod and Gun Club meet on the second Tuesday of each month in Building 1723, on B Street between 1st and 2nd Streets. Facilities include a skeet range, and a store with both hunting and fishing supplies.

HOBBY SHOPS--DM has six well-equipped hobby shops, offering the retiree opportunities in everything from auto repair, ceramic-making, TV repair to woodworking in one of the finest shops anywhere.

COMMUNITY CENTER--A 'home-away-from-home,' the DM Community Center sponsors numerous social and recreational events on a regular basis, and is amply equipped with facilities for activities ranging from games to music appreciation. Authorized persons can buy discount cards for Disneyland and Sea World at the Center.

Tickets for local sporting events and bullfights in Nogales, Mexico are also available at the Center, and patrons can obtain travel and recreation information about the Tucson area as well as the Western states.

FORT HUACHUCA

Founded in 1877 as a cavalry outpost to protect settlers in the area, Ft. Huachuca is the only one of the famous Territory of Arizona forts to survive into modern times. Official records state that the fort was retained after the Indian wars ended "because statistics showed it to be a remarkably healthy location, and because of continuing border troubles involving Indian renegades, Mexican bandits, and American outlaws and freebooters."

Located just 12 miles from the Mexican border at the base of the rugged Huachuca Mountains, the fort is 72 miles from Tucson and 19 miles from Tombstone. It encompasses over 73,000 acres and ranges in altitude from 4,000 to 8,000 feet. Summers are cool to warm, and winters are cold at night but mild on most days with lots of brilliant sunshine.

The scenery in the immediate vicinity of Ft. Huachuca is spectacular to say the least. The site was

an Indian village for more than a thousand years before the coming of Europeans. Huachuca is a Sobaipu-
ri Indian word meaning "Place of Thunder."

Ft. Huachuca is now the home of the U.S. Army Strategic Communications Command, and several other units
and services.

RETIREMENT SERVICES
The *Retirement Services Office (RSO)* at Ft. Huachuca (Building 22408, tel 538-3610) serves the interests
and needs of retired Army personnel and their families
thoughout the state, both before and after retirement.
The national headquarters of RSO publishes a newsletter which is sent to retired Army personnel.

Ft. Huachuca also has a comprehensive range of facilities and services that are available to retirees
and their families. These include the Raymond W. Bliss
Army Hospital, a commissary, main PX, Lakeside Officer's Club, a Service Club for enlisted personnel
active and retired, and an Aviation Club.

The fort also boasts a comparable range of recreational opportunities, including golf, tennis, shooting,
swimming, riding, bowling, arts and crafts, various
repair shops, picnic areas; plus access to three libraries and three movie theaters.

GUIDE BOOK
Military retirees interested in the facilities and
services available at Ft. Huachuca may pick up a copy
of a detailed guide on the fort that gives specific
details, including addresses, hours, phone numbers
and services.

VII

COST OF LIVING
TAXES & LAWS
IN ARIZONA

RETIREMENT LIVING BUDGETS

The cost of living for a retired couple in Phoenix, Scottsdale, Tempe, Mesa, Tucson, Sun City, Green Valley or any of the other popular Arizona communities has of course been rising steadily, along with the cost of everything else everywhere else.

Studies conducted by the Economic and Business Bureau of Arizona State University indicate that the increase in the cost of retirement living in the Phoenix area has, in fact, been faster than the national average--mostly because it was once well below the national average--and the area is no longer a "cheap retirement center."

How cheap or how expensive retirement living is in Arizona depends on dozens of variable factors, ranging from the size of the city, the area in the city, personal life-style preference, and so on.

In general terms, the Phoenix-Tucson areas now compare with retirement living in Atlanta, Buffalo, Boston and San Francisco; also with comparable smaller communities in outlying rural areas. As in most cases, retirees tailor their life-style to fit their income and what they are used to, and there are a range of choices in Arizona that will fit any reasonable budget.

HOUSING

Conventional housing in the moderate and expensive ranges is usually available in Greater Phoenix and Tucson, and the retirement cities and planned communities already covered generally have ample room for additional growth. Low-cost housing of the convention-

al type is scarce, however, and the few public and
private developments with low to moderately priced
housing are complete or have long waiting lists.

At the same time, housing in the Phoenix area
and the rest of Arizona is still a bargain when compared with the costs in many other parts of the country. Studies have shown that the housing dollar buys
more here than in most other sections of the nation
--despite the fact that the median cost of housing
has increased dramatically in the last decade.

For many retirees, the mobile home is the solution to economical housing. Mobile home dwellers account for nearly 15 percent of the home-owners in
the Valley of the Sun. Parks for mobile homes, travel trailers and combinations of both types are
plentiful, and often in surroundings that are scenic
and generally conducive to pleasant and convenient
living.

Before the retiring couple jumps into the mobile
home/travel trailer type of living, however, careful
checking on the dealerships and parks is highly recommended. Some parks have rules and regulations
that may add up to regimentation for some people.
Others are lacking in controls and may not have adequate upkeep programs. Care should also be taken
to avoid the unscrupulous and fly-by-night operator.
The best idea is to interview several of the residents in a park that appears interesting, in addition to checking with the local Better Business Bureau and Chambers of Commerce for any negative re-
ports.

FOOD & CLOTHING

Basically, food prices in Arizon are about the
same as those prevailing in other U.S. cities. As
in other locations, careful shopping combined with
buying in season and "on specials" along with ju-
dicious use of the freezer, will help keep food
bills below average. More and more retirees in outlying areas are resorting to planting gardens to
help keep their food bills down.

As elsewhere, the cost of clothing in Arizona is
largely a matter of taste and good shopping. Your

expenses can be kept to a minimum if you are not into
fashion wear and are content with the good, sturdy
clothing that can be had at non-prestige family stores
such as Yellow Front. In any event, lightweight casu-
al wear is in keeping with the life-style in Arizona.
Wise shoppers do their buying during clearance sales;
particularly those held right after Christmas, etc.

UTILITIES
    Electricity and natural gas are the prime power
and heating materials in Arizona. Gas is not as cheap
as it is in some states because it has to be piped in
from Texas and New Mexico. Monthly rates are far from
prohibitive, however. Electricity is about average in
cost.
    Although the cost of heating homes in winter is low
in the deserts and southern Arizona because of the
mild climate, this can be offset by the cost of air-
conditioning during the summer months. Two types of
cooling are in use in Arizona: refrigeration and evap-
oration. Refrigeration is the most effective and the
most expensive by far. As a result, many people are
going back to the evaporative system, which in the
meantime has been greatly improved over the earlier
units. The evaporative system is surprisingly effective when the humidity is low--and is a lot healthier
and preferable to many older people.
    The cost of water in Arizona varies from winter to
summer, and from household to household. Some people
have pools as well as gardens and use a lot. Generally speaking, water costs are low. Many homes in Greater Phoenix are built on former farm or orchard land
that had irrigation water rights. These homes still
have the same rights and periodically receive water
into their yards via underground pipes.

SALES & EXCISE TAXES
    The state assesses a sales tax of 4% on all pur-
chases, including food. The city of Phoenix and most
other Arizona municipalities assess an additional 1%
tax on food items as well as other purchases. Phoenix
still imposes a 1% sales tax on non-food items. Luxury taxes are imposed on liquor, cigarettes and other

tobacco products by the state and some cities. The
state levy on gasoline is 7-cents a gallon; the federal tax is 4-cents per gallon, for a total of 11-
cents.

ARIZONA STATE INCOME TAX
    In Arizona any individual with a net annual income
of $1,000 or over or a gross income of $5,000 or over
and any couple with a net annual income of $2,000 or
over or a gross income of $5,000 or over must file a
state income tax return.
    Under the *Arizona State Income Tax Code,* persons
65 years and over are granted an additional $1,000
personal exemption in filing their state income tax
returns. Persons 65 and older are also allowed medical and dental expenses without reference to the statutory limitation of $5,000 for a couple or $2,500
for a single person. If either the husband or wife is
over 65, medical expenses of both spouses are exempt-
ed from the limitations.
    If after all exemptions and deductions, the indi-
vidual or couple has net income above the statutory
limitations, then taxes varying from two to eight
percent of the net taxable income must be paid. If
the individual or couple must pay federal income tax,
the amount paid can be deducted from gross income before the state income tax is figured.
    In addition to these benefits, senior citizens may
get help in filing their returns from the various Tax
Commission offices.

AUTOMOBILE EMISSION TESTING
    In order to obtain a registration and license for
your automobile in Maricopa and Pima counties you
must have your car inspected for emission of pollu-
tants. Only cars 13 years old and older are exempt
from the regulation. To get your car tested you must
take it and a copy of the old registration to one of
the official inspection stations, listed in the White
Pages of the telephone directory under Vehicle Inspection Stations. Call the one nearest you for hours
of operation.
    The inspection report that you receive from the

Inspection Station must be included with your license renewal application. For other information, call the Arizona Health Department Vehicular Emission Control, at 255-5067, or Hamilton Test Systems, 943-7731.

AUTOMOBILE TAX

Newcomers moving to Arizona pay an $8 registration fee for each car they own. The cost of Arizona license plates is initially based on the maker's suggested retail price when the car is new. This fee remains the same for the first three years, then decreases in increments of three years until the auto is 10 years old. Thereafter it remains the same.

MOBILE HOME TAX

Mobile homes that are 8'x40' or bigger are taxed as unsecured personal property. Taxes are based on 82% of the suggested retail price of the manufacturer when the home was new, and gradually decrease to 15% of this value over a period of 15 years. Mobile homes that are smaller than 8'x40' are taxed as automobiles and require license plates.

ESTATE TAXES

There is a basic exemption of $100,000 on the net estate of an Arizona resident who dies. The net estate is defined by law, and is the difference between the total value of the gross estate and the total statutory deductions. Statutory deductions include: expenses of the last illness; funeral expenses; expenses incurred in administering property subject to claims; debts of the decedent; net losses during administration; expenses incurred in administering property not subject to claim; bequests, etc. to surviving spouse.

If a non-resident decedent owns real property in Arizona, the exemption and deductions are pro-rated in the ratio which the Arizona state bears to the entire estate where it is situated. There is no gift tax in Arizona.

The rates of estate tax imposed by Arizona law is 80 percent of the basic Federal rates. Returns on taxable estates must be filed with the Estate Tax Department, 1700 W. Washington, Phoenix, Az 85007, tel 255-4424, within 15 months after death. In appraising estates, the valuation as of the date of death or the optional evaluation one year after death may be used. Interest at the rate of six percent a year is charged if the tax is not paid within the 15-month period. If an extension of time for payment has been granted by the Tax Commissioner, an interest rate of four percent is charged against the unpaid tax.

The Estate Tax Department is also the agency that gives official approval for the release of the contents of safe deposit boxes and all bank accounts in excess of $5,000, as well as standing waivers on real estate or any stock standing in the names of deceased persons.

For those who are interested in more detailed information, the Estate Tax Commission publishes a booklet spelling out the various laws and regulations. The booklet is available free from the Estate Tax Department of Arizona, 1700 W. Washington, Phoenix, Az 85007. As for a copy of the *Estate Tax Laws of Arizona and Regulations*.

PROPERTY TAX

Property taxes in Arizona vary according to the county, city or town and district. As a rule, the base for residential property tax is an assessment of approximately 88 percent of the property's full cash value, times 15 percent. The resulting figure is then applied against the tax rate effective in that particular district.

There is a credit on Property Tax available to anyone 65 or older who meets certain criteria. For information and forms, contact the Arizona State Department of Revenue, tel 255-4269, and request Form 140-PTC. The form contains complete instructions and qualifications for the Property Tax Credit.

TAX TIPS FOR THE RETIRED

There are many tax laws; they change frequently, and there is a different set of laws for those who are 65 and older. Most of the special tax benefits available to retired persons are explained in a booklet entitled *Tax Benefits for Older Americans,* available

free at Internal Revenue Service offices or for 20¢
from the Superintendent of Documents, U.S. Government Printing Office, Washington, D.C. 20402. Ask for
Publication No. 554.

FREE TAX AID

In the Phoenix area, retirees whose income is
$20,000 or under and consists of salaries, wages,
tips, dividends, interest, pension or annuities, can
get their federal income tax computed free by the
Phoenix office of the IRS--if you take the standard
deductions.

COMMUNITY PROPERTY LAWS

Arizona is a Community Property state. This means
that real or personal property acquired by either
spouse during marriage is the common property of both.
If property was owned separately by one spouse before
moving to Arizona, however, the title to and any income accruing from the property remains separate.

DRIVER'S LICENSES

The driver's license fee in Arizona is $5. All ap-
plicants must take a written test on traffic regulations and have eye examinations. Those applying for
a license in Arizona for the first need not take a
driver's test if they have a valid license from some
other state. Driver's licenses are obtained from the
Motor Vehicle Division of the Arizona State Highway
Department. See the telephone directory for the location nearest you.

DIVORCE LAWS

For a divorce in Arizona the law requires residence of one year in the state and at least six months in the county where the action is filed.

HOMEOWNER PROTECTION

Warranties on new homes or additions to old ones
are usually good for only one year. It is therefore
important that a careful inspection of any new home
or structure be made within the first year. There is,
however, some added protection. Under Arizona law
you may file a complaint against a contractor any
time within two years after the workd is completed.

Such complaints are filed through the Registrar of Contractors at 1818 W. Adams in Phoenix, and 415 W. Congress in Tucson.

JURY DUTY

Persons 65 or older receive no preferential treatment as far as jury duty is concerned in Arizona. You may, however, follow the normal procedures for exemption from jury duty that is allowed all citizens.

MARRIAGE LAWS

In Arizona a couple may marry or remarry without a waiting period provided they have had a blood test not more than 32 days or less than 48 hours prior to issuance of the license, and any divorce awarded in another state is final.

MOTOR VEHICLE REGISTRATION & PLATES

As soon as you become an Arizona resident you are required to obtain Arizona license plates for your car. Licenses are issued by the Motor Vehicle Division of the Department of Transportation (for the address nearest you, see Automobile Registration-Plates under the county listings in the telephone book).

When applying for your license, you must present the previous registration card, title or bill of sale and any lien documents. Your vehicle will be inspected to verify identity and ownership, and you must turn in your out-of-state plates when you get your new ones. Fees vary according to the year, make and model of your car. See Automobile Emission Testing in this chapter.

Winter visitors and tourists vacationing in Arizona may stay indefinitely without getting Arizona license plates for their cars, as long as they do not become residents of the state.

RECKLESS DRIVING

Arizona is one of the states using the point system to penalize drivers for traffic violations. Any person who accumulates eight points in any 12-month period is subject to loss of license. Four different traffic violations can cause you to lose your license as a result of just one accident. These are: driving

under the influence of alcohol; reckless driving
while under the influence of alcohol; reckless driving, and drag-racing in the streets. The penalty for
speeding is 3 points; for leaving the scene of an
accident or hit-and-run, six points. All other moving
violations are two points each.

Newcomers, especially those from California, should
keep in mind that even though pedestrians in Arizona
have the right-of-way, this right is not very well o-
beyed or enforced. During peak traffic hours older
people especially are cautioned to cross streets only
at designated crossings.

PET LAWS
State laws require that dogs owned by residents of
Arizona be vaccinated against rabies, and licensed.
The licensing fee is $10. Out-of-state licenses are
valid until you establish Arizona residence. Neither
licenses or vaccinations are required for cats. Contact the nearest county Veterinary Center.

VOTING IN ARIZONA
For detailed information about voting in Arizona,
contact the *League of Women Voters of Arizona* and ask
for a copy of their *ABCs of Voting in Arizona*. In the
Phoenix area call 946-7159 or write P.O. Box 7662,
Phoenix, Az 85011. In Tucson, call the Voter Registration Division, County Recorder's Office, 115 N.
Church, tel 792-8101, or the Election Board at 792-
8408.

Any person of age who has been in Arizona for 30
days prior to an election is eligible to register and
vote. Anyone 65 or older is allowed to vote by absentee ballot by reason of age alone. A qualified and
registered voter who wants to vote absentee must apply to the County Recorder for an absentee ballot.

PARKING FOR THE HANDICAPPED
In Arizona most free parking lots--at shopping centers, hospitals and banks, etc.--reserve a number of
spaces for the physically handicapped. These spaces
are usually among those nearest the store or office
entrances, and are designated by a symbol of a person

sitting in a wheelchair. If you are handicapped, you may obtain a special license plate bearing the same wheelchair symbol to show that you are eligible to use the reserved space.

To obtain an application for one of the special plates, contact the nearest office of the Arizona Department of Transportation, Motor Vehicle Division, Auto License Plates.

VIII

RECREATION & LEISURE-TIME OPPORTUNITIES IN ARIZONA

THE OUTDOOR LIFE

As in so many other areas of life in Arizona, the style and quality of recreation and leisure-time activities in the state is primarily determined by the weather, and secondarily by the desert and mountain terrain. The super-abundance of year-around sunshine and benevolent temperatures in the desert regions, along with the distinctive geography, not only encourages leisure-time activities but also orients them toward the outside.

Golfing, swimming, boating, horseback riding, fishing, tennis, hiking, rockhounding, bicycling, overnight camping, sightseeing, backyard barbecuing, pool partying....are just a few of the pleasureable pursuits to which Arizonans devote a great deal of time.

The same factors that entice Arizonans outside to relax and play in the sun have also made the state a major market for tourism. Both of these influences combined have resulted in the availability of an extraordinary volume and variety of facilities for active leisure--over and above the natural ones provided by the mountains, canyons, rivers, lakes and hundreds of square miles of living desert.

There are numerous sources of detailed information on Arizona's leisure-time opportunities. These include, of course, the local chambers of commerce and many books and maps produced by Phoenix Books and other publishers. A free brochure on *Books and Maps on Arizona* may be obtained from the publisher of this book.

CHAMBERS OF COMMERCE

For visitor-oriented information about Arizona you may also contact the following chambers:

Apache Junction, P.O. Box 101, Apache Junction, Az 85220. Tel 982-3141

Buckeye, Box 717, Buckeye, Az 85326. Tel 386-2727

Bullhead City, Box 66, Bullhead City, Az 86430. Tel 754-8891

Carefree & Cave Creek, c/o Carefree Center, Carefree, Az 85331. Tel 488-3381

Casa Grande, 201 E. 4th St., Casa Grande, Az 85222. Tel 836-2125

Chandler, 201 E. Commonwealth Ave., Chandler, Az 85224. Tel 963-4571

Cottonwood/Verde Valley, P.O. Box 412, Cottonwood, Az 86326. Tel 634-2912

Eloy, 508 N. Main St., Eloy, Az 85231. Tel 466-7353

Flagstaff, Box 1150, Flagstaff, Az 86001. Tel 744-4505

Glendale, 7125 N. 58th Dr., Glendale, Az 85301. Tel 937-4754

Goodyear/Litchfield Park, 113 E. Western Ave., Avondale, Az 85323. Tel 932-2260

Holbrook/Petrified Forest, 324 Navajo Blvd., Holbrook, Az 86025. Tel 524-6558.

Lake Havasu City, Box 707, Lake Havasu City, Az 86403. Tel 855-4115.

Page/Lake Powell, Box 727, Page, Az 86040. Tel 645-2741

Payson, Drawer A, Payson, Az 85541. Tel 474-2595

Peoria, 8265 N. Grand Ave., Peoria, Az 85345. Tel 979-3601

Mesa, Drawer C, Mesa, Az 85201. Tel 969-1307

Phoenix, 34 W. Monroe, Phoenix, Az 85003. Tel 254-5521.

Prescott, Box 1147, Prescott, Az 86301. Tel 445-2000

Scottsdale, 7333 Main St., Scottsdale, Az 85251. Tel 945-8481

Sedona/Oak Creek, Box 478, Sedona, Az 86336. Tel 282-7722

Springerville/White Mountains, Box 181, Springerville, Az 85938. Tel 333-4321.

Tempe, 508 E. Southern Dr., Tempe, Az 85281. Tel 967-
  7891
Tombstone, Box 67, Tombstone, Az 85638. Tel 457-3552
Tucson, 420 W. Congress, Tucson, Az 85701. Tel 624-
  8111
Wickenburg, P.O. Drawer CC, Wickenburg, Az 85358.
  Tel 684-5479
Yuma, Box 230, Yuma, Az 85364. Tel 782-2567

PHOENIX VISITORS' & CONVENTION BUREAU

Each year there are over 500 annual events in the
Valley of the Sun, and another 200 or more in Tucson,
Flagstaff, Tombstone, Prescott, Wickenburg, Parker,
Window Rock, Sells and other Arizona cities and towns.
These events range from rodeos and pow wows to boat
races and musical festivals. The best source of infor-
mation about these events is the *Phoenix Convention &
Visitors' Bureau* at 2701 E. Camelback Rd., Suite 200-
H, Phoenix, Az 85016. Tel (602) 957-0070.

PARKS & RECREATION DEPARTMENTS

Each city maintains a Parks and Recreation Department that administers the parks, swimming pools, and
other city-owned recreational and cultural facilities
that are available, and all have various on-going programs ranging from arts and crafts to sporting events.

For details about both the facilities and events
in your area, contact the local Parks and Recreation
Department under the city listings. Many of the de-
partments publish annual activities and facilities
guides that are available to the public.

FISHING IN ARIZONA

Despite its huge desert areas and mountainous terrain, Arizona is famous for its fishing—in numerous
rivers and manmade lakes. There are a variety of regulations concerning licenses, areas and seasons, but
the rules are quite reasonable. For detailed information, write or call the Arizona Game & Fish Department (I&E Division), 2222 W. Greenway Rd., Phoenix,
Az 85023, tel 942-3000, and ask for one of their
Hunting & Fishing in Arizona brochures.

Anyone who has lived in Arizona for 25 years or more and is 70 years old and above may obtain hunting and fishing licenses free.

"GOLDEN AGE" PARK PASSPORTS
Persons 62 years of age and older may obtain free *Golden Age* passes to the nation's federal parklands, which abound in Arizona. The permits may be obtained at all national park entrances where fees are charged. Applications for the passes must be made in person, and proof of age must be presented. The permit allows the entry of the holder and any person accompanying him or her in a private vehicle. At developed federal recreational areas where fees are charged for using camping facilities, etc., senior citizens with Golden Age passes receive a 50 percent discount.

TELEPHONE PARKCAST
You can get up-to-date information about Arizona's many national parks by telephoning (Phoenix area) 258-4511. A tape-recorded message prepared by the National Park Service gives information and current weather conditions, admission prices and hours of operation. Besides this general information, an individual park is featured each week on the tapes. If you need other information about national parks, call 261-4956 (also a Phoenix number).

OTHER RECREATIONAL OPPORTUNITIES
Arizona offers more opportunities for more sporting and recreational activities than several states combined. About the only thing you cannot do in Arizona is go deep-sea fishing--and you can do that in nearby Mexico in the Gulf of California.

There are more golf courses in Arizona than in Ireland where the game was invented. Tennis courts abound. There are riding stables, running clubs, bicycling organizations--you name it and there are thousands of people who do it. The camping, hiking and sightseeing opportunities are virtually unlimited. For a comprehensive guide, see Bob Golden's *Outdoor Recreation in Arizona*, available from Phoenix Books.

For current news about water sports in Arizona,
you will find *Arizona Waterways,* the Southwest's
leading watersports newspaper, both interesting and
useful. It is published monthly by Arizona Waterways,
537 S. Stone Ave., Tucson, Az 85701, tel 792-1124,
and is available state-wide at marine stores and bait
shops.

SURVIVING IN THE DESERT

Notwithstanding their great natural beauty and benign appearance--especially from the comfort of an
air-conditioned car--Arizona's deserts can be danger-
ous, even fatal, to the unprepared and unwary. It is
amazingly easy to get lost in the desert when you are
just a few hundred yards away from a highway or your
starting point. Furthermore, it is not uncommon for
cars to breakdown, and even if you are on a fairly
well-traveled road it may be hours before you are re-
scued.

Especially in mid-summer but at other times as
well, the low humidity and heat of the desert sun
causes very rapid body dehydration, so it is vital to
follow a number of rules when you are traveling in,
sightseeing, rock-hunting or whatever in the state's
large desert areas. The danger is real enough that
each year there are usually a number of deaths when
people become lost or stranded in a dry, isolated
area. To help prevent such tragedies, there are a number of survival rules that should be made routine for
any desert outing. These include:

1) Never go very far into the desert or travel on
an interstate highway without water for drinking and
for your car radiator. Plastic bottles or jugs make
excellent lightweight containers for water.

2) Before going into the desert on a hike or sightseeing trip, etc., always tell someone that you are
going; tell them where you are going and how long
you expect to be gone. Leave them a description of
your car, and your license number.

3) If you drive into the desert and get lost, or
have car trouble and are many miles from known help,
stay with your car. A car is easier to find and

affords some protection from the daytime sun and night-
time chill.

4) If you are on foot and become completely lost,
keep your clothes on to slow the rate of water evapor-
ation from your body; provide yourself with some kind
of shade, and stay where you are until help comes.
Avoid sitting or lying directly on the ground, because
it may be as much as 30 degrees hotter than a foot a-
bove ground.

5) If you have water, drink until you are satisfied for as long as the water lasts. Rationing water
when the temperature is high and the humidity is low
is inviting disaster. Loss of efficiency and collapse
always follow dehydration.

6) Breathe through your nose and avoid talking.
Do not drink any alcohol or take any salt. Delay eat-
ing any food unless you have plenty of water to go
with it.

*It is also a good idea to keep an emergency kit in
your car glove compartment.*

VISITING MEXICO

Mexico, which has one of the world's most colorful
and fascinating cultures, borders Arizona on the south,
and is a favorite mecca for vacationers, shoppers,
fishermen, campers, gourmets and lovers. During holidays, on ordinary weekends and during summer vacations
thousands of Arizona residents and visitors flock to
the border towns and the resort cities along Mexico's
famous *Gold Coast* facing the Sea of Cortez (Gulf of
California).

These popular sea-side resorts begin with Santa
Clara south of Yuma, and include Puerto Penasco (Rock-
y Point) south of Gringo Pass (Lukeville); Nogales,
across from Nogales, Arizona; Kino Bay, west of Hermosillo; San Carlos Bay, south of Hermosillo; Guay-
mas, adjoining San Carlos; Topolobampo further south,
and exciting Mazatlan.

It is very easy for Americans to enter Mexico. No
documentation, approval or permission of any type is
necessary to visit the border towns of San Luis,

Sonoita, Nogales, Naco or Agua Prieta. There is no
limit to the number of times you can cross the border or stay on the Mexican side of the border--as long
as you do not go more than 25 miles from the border
itself.

If you want to travel into the interior of Mexico
it is necessary to obtain a *Tourist Card* from a Mexican Consulate or Mexican Government Tourist Office,
or from the Mexican Immigration Office where you cross
the border. There is no charge for these permits and
you can usually get them in just a few minutes unless
you happen to hit a rush period, such as just before
a holiday or a weekend.

In applying for a Tourist Card you need proof of
citizenship. A birth certificate, military discharge
papers, voting certificate, passport, or notorized
affidavit of nationality is acceptable. A driver's
license is not acceptable.

In Arixona Mexican Tourist Cards are available
from the National Tourist Council at 5151 E. Broadway, Tucson. Tel 745-5055. Remember that the office
may be closed for lunch until 2 p.m.

For a comprehensive guide to visiting this part
of Mexico see *Mexico's West Coast Beaches,* by Al &
Mildred Fischer, available from Phoenix Books for
$4.95.

IX

ORGANIZATIONS & PUBLICATIONS OF INTEREST TO SENIOR CITIZENS

ASCA NEWS & BUDGETEER

The official publication of the Arizona Senior Citizens' Association, the *ASCA NEWS* carries information about local, state and national services, events and developments that are of special interest to senior citizens. The *Shoppers Money Budgeteer,* which accompanies the News as an insert, features money-saving coupons, gift offers, cash refunds and free products available from companies all over the country.

There are three categories of membership in the ASCA: senior citizens (anyone 55 or older), regular members (anyone under 55), and associate members (business firms and other commercial enterprises with products or services to sell to senior citizens).

Annual ASCA membership rates for senior citizens are quite low, as are the fees for other membership categories. All members receive copies of the News and the Budgeteer, both of which are useful bargains.

ASCA is an independent, non-profit organization that depends upon memberships and advertising revenue for its existence. It addition to publishing the News and Budgeteer, the Association acts as a referral center for associate members offering home repair and other professional services to members.

For more information about ASCA and application forms, write to the Association at 9226 N. 7th St., Phoenix, Az 85020, or call 997-2225.

ARIZONA SENIOR WORLD

Senior World is a monthly tabloid-sized newspaper aimed at informing, serving and entertaining senior citizens, and is one of the best publications in the

state that is totally devoted to the interests of older adults. It is available by subscription or may be
picked up free at hundreds of distribution points
around the state (markets, adult centers, etc.).

A subsidiary of Senior World Publications of San
Diego, the Arizona edition of Senior World is head-
quartered at 1807 N. Central Ave., Pheonix, Az 85004,
Suite 108. Tel 252-1793.

PHOENIX LIVING MAGAZINE
Published especially for people thinking about moving into the Phoenix area, *Phoenix Living Magazine*
covers homes, apartments, shopping, entertainment, recreational and cultural facilities, and more. It also
features maps of different sections of the Valley basin, showing the locations of specific homes and a-
partments.

Phoenix Living is published bi-monthly and is circulated via newsstands, drug stores, supermarkets,
chambers of commerce, visitor centers and large companies in the area. Publisher is Baker Publications,
Inc., Suite 305, 4621 N. 16th St., Phoenix, Az 85016.
Tel 279-2394.

AMERICAN ASSOCIATION OF RETIRED PERSONS
The *American Association of Retired Persons (AARP)*
was founded in 1958 as a counterpart to the National
Retired Teachers Association. Today AARP is the largest and most influential national organization concerned with the interests and problems of people who
are 55 and older, whether retired or not. The association currently has over 12 million members.

Those interested in joining AARP should write to
its national headquarters at 1909 K Street, N.W.,
Washington, D.C. 20049. The annual fee of $4 covers
both husband and wife.

For this fee, members of AARP receive two publications: the bi-monthly magazine *Modern Maturity* and
the monthly *AARP News Bulletin;* the opportunity to
buy prescription medicines and other medical needs at
reasonable prices through a mail-service pharmacy;
reduced rates at a number of hotel and motel chains
and rental car companies; and the chance to join the

NRTA-AARP Motoring Plan, the only nationwide automo-
tive club designed specifically to meet the needs of
older drivers.

With a legislative staff in Washington, D.C. and
volunteer legislative committees in all 50 states,
AARP provides older Americans with a vigorous voice
on issues affecting their welfare. The association
has been in the forefront of efforts to end age discrimination and mandatory retirement, to reform Social Security and Medicare, to develop a comprehensive
national health insurance program for all Americans,
and to improve housing and transportation programs
throughout the nation.

Another AARP priority is community service. The
more than 3,000 AARP chapters around the country
(the first was incorporated in Youngtown, Arizona in
1960) undertake a wide range of worthwhile service
projects each year--including programs in health education, income tax assistance, crime prevention,
consumer education, church relations, and driver improvement.

AARP members also serve as individuals in numerous local projects such as meals-on-wheels, Foster
Grandparent and Retired Senior Volunteer programs.

A division of AARP, Action for Independent Maturity (AIM), has pioneered in the field of pre-retirement planning. With over half a million members
between 50 and 65, AIM's primary goal is to help
middle-aged Americans prepare for successful retirement. AIM's special retirement planning seminar is
being used by major corporations, government agencies, colleges and universities, and professional
groups for their employees or members.

Arizona residents who are members of AARP and want
to take advantage of its pharmacy service should send
their prescriptions to: Nevada Retired Persons Pharmacy, 5947 Boulder Highway, East Las Vegas, Nevada
89112.

When ordering for the first time, you must send
the original prescription--not a copy. Make sure that
your doctor indicates the number of refills authorized. When ordering refills, use the prescription

number assigned by the Pharmacy Service that is print-
ed on the label. Do not send money with your order.
You will be billed. There is no charge for postage unless you request special delivery.

NATIONAL COUNCIL OF SENIOR CITIZENS

The *National Council of Senior Citizens (NCSC)* was
organized in 1961 by Aime J. Forand, a retired Cong-
ressman from Rhode Island, and spearheaded the cam-
paign that resulted in the formation of Medicare. The
NCSC's goals are to promote stronger social security
and better housing for the elderly, and to provide
jobs for the low-income elderly. The organization also
undertakes to fight discrimination against senior citizens, and to serve as a link between the elderly
and other large national organizations.

The NCSC platform covers income, health, housing,
employment, nutrition, transportation, education,
planning, research and demonstration, retirement roles
and activities, training, facilities-programs-ser-
vices, Government and non-Government organization, and
spiritual well-being.

The *Senior Citizen News,* published by NCSC monthly,
is one of the best newspapers in the field. The organization also has life and death insurance, drug programs and tour programs. It has a network of affili-
ates across the country.

For more information and membership applications,
write the National Council of Senior Citizens, 1511 K
Street, N.W., Washington, D.C. 20005. The name and
telephone number of the Arizona representative of the
NCSC may be obtained from the Area Agency on Aging,
tel 264-2255.

NAT'L ASSOCIATION OF RETIRED FEDERAL EMPLOYEES

NARFE, as this association is called, was organized in the late 1920s by a group of 14 men who recognized the need for united effort in providing a
spokesman for retirees of the federal government. The
association now has over 1,000 chapters in all 50
states, with some 200,000 members.

NARFE has been a major advocate for updating and
liberalizing the Civil Service Retirement Law. As a

voice for senior citizens NARFE is greatly interested
in the wide scope of problems of the aged and aging,
and is active in pre-retirement counseling throughout the Government service.

Like AARP and the NCSC, NARFE membership includes
eligibility for a comprehensive group insurance program, and drug and tour services. Low national dues
include a subscription to the Association's monthly
magazine *Retirement Life*.

Arizona is one of the five states in Region VII
that has a NARFE state federation encompassing all
the local chapters. There are five chapters in the
Valley of the Sun--in Phoenix, Sun City/Youngtown,
Mesa, Scottsdale and Apache Junction. Information
about NARFE, on both a local and national level, can
be obtained by contacting NARFE, 1909 Q Street, N.W.
Washington, D.C. 20009.

TELEPHONE PIONEERS OF AMERICA

Retirees of the Bell Telephone system are eligible for membership in the *Telephone Pioneers of America,* a nationwide organization which is active in a
variety of community projects. The Phoenix Life Member Club is affiliated with Coronado Chapter No. 66,
which covers Arizona, New Mexico and El Paso. Further information is available from the Secretary-
Treasurer of the Coronado Chapter, P.O. Box 2320,
Phoenix, Az 85002.

ARIZONA COUNCIL FOR SENIOR CITIZENS

In addition to seeking to influence state legislation on behalf of the elderly, the ACSC also promotes the organization of senior citizen councils on
a county level and helps to coordinate their activities.

Among the specific goals of the Arizona Council
for Senior Citizens: to acquaint all senior citizens
in the state with the issues at stake; with the government officials in office and candidates running
for office; to encourage the elderly to register and
to vote for candidates who have shown themselves to
be favorable toward the needs of the elderly; to
help develop programs and services for senior citizens

on a county-by-county basis; to strive to achieve better housing and transportation facilities for low-income retirees; to obtain legislation that would re-
duce the tax burden imposed on less than affluent senior citizens.

Newcomers in Arizona and new retirees interested
in contributing to the efforts of their local county
senior citizen's council or the state council are invited to contact the Area Agency on Aging for the
phone numbers of current officers. Tel (Phoenix) 264-
2255.

ARIZONA VETERANS' SERVICE COMMISSION

The *Arizona Veterans' Service Commission* maintains
field offices in Phoenix, Tucson, Yuma and Flagstaff.
These offices serve as advocates of veterans' benefits. They administer the benefits and provide the
services authorized by law for veterans, their dependents and beneficiaries. The Service also acts as
the guardian of the estates of incompetent veterans
under provisions of the Uniform Veterans Guardianship
Act.

AUTO INSURANCE POLICY CANCELLATION

The *State of Arizona Department of Insurance* provides a service to elderly residents by making sure
the statutes covering the cancellation of auto insurance are observed. These statutes provide that no
insurance can be cancelled solely because of the holder's age. They also require that the insuring company
must advise the policy holder of his right to com-
plain if his policy is cancelled for any reason.

INSURANCE INTERPRETATION & CLAIMS SERVICE

The Arizona Department of Insurance also operates
a *Complaint Department* which comes to the aid of the
elderly in matters concerning insurance interpretat-
ion, claims and benefits--in some cases involving
policies bought as long as 30 years ago. The Department has out-of-office investigators to help people
who cannot leave their homes. It has subpoena pow-
ers and access to legal assistance when needed. The
Insurance Department of Arizona is located at 1601 W.
Jefferson, Phoenix, Az 85007. Tel 255-5448.

ACHIEVING AFTER RETIREMENT

In 1970 retired postal employee Francis Ervay
founded an Arizona organization he called *Retirement
Achievements* to help the retired person with the dif-
icult task of recycling himself or herself back into
life as a contributing member of the community. The
organization is now inactive because of lack of support, but Ervay was and remains one of the few seminal thinkers in the area of problems and interests of
older individuals in America today.

Ervay's theme is that for the most part, solutions
to the problems of the retired have been sought within a framework of dependency--an approach "that has
failed to conserve, mobilize or use the experience of
the older people in the task of improving the quality
of American life." Ervay says that the 'solutions'
so far have in fact made the problems of the retired
and aged segment of the American population more ser-
ious--not the least of which is the welfare burden
which has increased several hundred percent since the
1960s.

"Dependency on the government is not a valid basis
for solving the problems of the retired generation.
The healthy older person can and must be given the
opportunity to continue using his skills and his ini-
tiative to contribute to society after retiring from
his salaried employment," Ervay states.

Ervay notes that ths New Generation of retired Americans is made up of three distinct categories: (1)
The very old, the weak, the sick and the handicapped--
who constitute about 47 percent of the total; (2) the
self-employed and the leaders, who make up only four
percent of the total; and (3) the newly retired mid-
dle and lower class who are fit and vigorous, and
who make up the remaining 49 percent of the total retired population.

There are many programs to help the people in Group
1, and the services for them are increasing in quanti-
ty and quality. Those in Group 2, the still employed
and the affluent, don't need any help. Group 3 is the
Lost Generation of this age. Absolute, utter boredom
is the fate of many. Their greatest need is creativity

and productivity, Ervay says. He adds: "In general,
older Americans are stereotyped as a class of people
who are dependents of society, who must be taken care
of and told what to do because they cannot fend for
themselves. With this concept for a start, it is only
a short step to the false assumption that all retired
people are no longer capable of producing and that
they should be converted to consumers of entertainment."

Ervay observes that the retired population of the
U.S. is increasing at the rate of about 400 thousand
a year, and that about half of the number who retire
each year are able-bodied, alert and active--and can
expect to live another 15 to 20 years."Yet most step
out--or are shoved out--of the mainstream of life;
the decades of their accumulated experience and wisdom thereafter going to waste. As a result of the prevailing system, roughly half of the retired people in
the U.S. are so silent and so lacking in clear-cut
identity that they are totally invisible--despite the
fact that retirees are big business, contributing
millions of dollars to the communities in which they
live."

Ervay's position is that the present general concept of retirement is misguided, not only socially
and economically, but legally as well. "The various
laws pertaining to Social Security, for example,
virtually forces many older people to stay out of in-
dustry. The law is used as a sword over their necks
to prevent them from doing things.

"Social agencies tend to treat retirees as wards
of the government, and to regard themselves as watch-
dogs whose job it is to keep the retired in line.
Social Security is not unearned welfare or a special
privilege. It is something that the retired person
has paid for during a life-time of working--like insurance. But he has no control over it.

"The present generation of retirees has contribut-
ed more to the growth and development of this country
than any generation in history. But its members are
being isolated in a passive life lacking in self-
fulfillment, in a sense of purpose. This New Generat-

ion and society are both losers in this waste of human resources."

Ervay's approach is for retirees to help themselves and others as well by starting new enterprises,
marketing new products and services...doing work
that the community needs done--"which would increase
their sense of value, add to their income and move
them back into the mainstream of community life."

Ervay presently operates a job-clearing service
(Serv-Yu) for retirees who need to supplement their
income by doing part-time or odd jobs. Serv-Yu rece-
ives a commission that ranges from 6 to 15 percent.
Contact: Serv-Yu, 2632 Foote Dr., Phoenix, Az 85008.
Tel 956-5620.

PROJECT FIND

This is a program of the Department of Agriculture aimed at locating senior citizens who need and
are eligible for food assistance. The project is also concerned with identifying other needs senior
citizens may have. Local Red Cross offices cooperate
with the project.

OTHER PUBLICATIONS OF INTEREST

A GUIDE TO BUDGETING FOR THE RETIRED COUPLE--Pre-
pared by the Consumer & Food Economics Research Division of the Agricultural Research Service, and
available from: Superintendent of Documents, U.S.
Government Printing Office, Washington, D.C. 20402.
Price 10¢. Order No. 0100-1518.

ARIZONA MOBILE CITIZEN--A weekly newspaper published for all Arizona mobile home owners, parks and
dealers by Arizona Trailer Publications, 4110 E. Van
Buren, Phoenix, Az 85008. Tel 275-2822. Full of news
and advertisements of interest to those who live in
mobile home parks. Also serves as a retail outlet
for mobile home park supplies, such as signs, receipt
books, registration cards, etc.

MOBILE MESSENGER--Another weekly newspaper serving
mobile home residents in Phoenix, Scottsdale, Tempe,
Mesa, Chandler, Gilbert and Apache Junction. Published by the Valley of the Sun Newspaper, P.O. Box 809,

Apache Junction, Az 85220. Tel 966-7244.

BETTER RETIREMENT GUIDES--These booklets represent a complete library of retirement living. Included are: Information, Consumer, Legal, Money, Anti-
Crime, Health, Activities, Housing, Home Repair, Safety, Psychology, Food, Pet, Widowhood, Income Tax,
Job, and State Tax guides. Individual copies of the
booklets are available free from AARP, P.O. Box 2240,
Long Beach, Calif. 90801.

AARP NEWS BULLETIN--Published monthly, the AARP
News Letter carries timely articles on legislative
developments, current events, community service activities by AARP chapters and individuals, and other
topics of interest to the elderly. Comes with membership in AARP.

DYNAMIC YEARS--A bi-monthly magazine, this is the
only national publication specifically designed for
working Americans in their middle-years who are interested in planning for successful retirement. It
comes with membership in Action for Independent
Maturity (AIM), the pre-retirement division of AARP.

MEDICARE & HEALTH INSURANCE FOR OLDER PEOPLE--
This is a detailed 24-page booklet that provies information about the Medicare program and various
types of supplemental health insurance. It includes
a consumer checklist to help consumers compare ele-
ments of various insurance policies along with warn-
ings about problems and abuses in the sale of such
insurance. Individual copies are available free from
AARP, Dept. M-H, P.O. Box 2400, Long Beach, Calif.
90801.

MODERN MATURITY--Another bi-monthly AARP publication, Modern Maturity is one of the nation's most
widely circulated magazines and probably the best-
known of the magazines for senior citizens. It features articles by leading authors, tips on retirement living, plus humorous and nostalgic pieces. It
comes with membership in AARP.

SOCIAL & CULTURAL ACTIVITIES GUIDE--Published

each year by the City of Phoenix Parks & Recreation
Department, this guide gives a detailed schedule of
the many social and cultural events sponsored by the
Department. The booklet is free and may be obtained
by calling at the Information Desk in the main lobby
of the Municipal Building, 251 W. Washington, in
downtown Phoenix.

CITY OF PHOENIX DIRECTORY OF SERVICES & INFORMAT-
ION--A small folder that is nevertheless a comprehensive guide to the services provided by the city
of Phoenix. The information is in alphabetical order
and covers everything from abandoned vehicles, age
cards, barking dogs, animal sanitation, building inspection, bus service, construction noise, fences,
illegal dumping, odor problems and social problems
to taxes. It's available at the Municipal Building,
251 W. Washington.

HARVEST YEARS--A monthly magazine published by
Harvest Years Publishing Co., 104 E. 40th St., New
York, NY 10016. The same house also produces several
pamphlets for retirees: Better Health, Financial
Planning, How to Earn Money in Retirement, How to
Guard Against Frauds and Quacks, How to Live Longer,
The Law, Retirement Housing, Retirement Spending
Guide, Creative Years, etc.

SOUTHERN ARIZONA FISHING GUIDE--Available from
Two-Sons Publishing Co., P.O. Box 3733, College Station, Tucson 85722. $2.50.

DIRECTORY OF ARIZONA GOLF COURSES--Published by
the Arizona Golf Association, P.O. Box 13236. Phoenix,
Arizona 85002. In addition to a list of member courses in the state, the directory also lists special
golfing events. Send $1 for packaging and postage.

PEOPLE'S YELLOW PAGES (OF TUCSON)--One of the most
interesting and useful publications one could have
on any city, the *People's Yellow Pages (of Tucson)*
is more than yellow-page listings. It is an encyclo-
pedia of the human services, artisans and alternat-
ives available in the Tucson area. There should be

a copy in every home. It is published annually by New
West Trails Collective, c/o the Tucson Ecumenical
Council, 715 Park, Tucson, Az 85719. It is available at
book stores, churches and other outlets in Tucson,
also by mail-order from the above address. Send $3.50.

PLANNING FOR TOMORROW KIT—-Available from 50-Plus
Magazine, 850 Third Ave., New York, NY 10022. $11.

READY OR NOT HANDBOOK—-From Manpower Education Institute 127 E. 35th St., New York, NY 10016. $4.50.

BEWARE OF CON-MEN

Home repair con-artists prey on anyone but their
favorite victims are the elderly. The Arizona Department of Public Safety warns retirees to beware of
these con-men—-who flock to Arizona during the winter
months especially.

Among the more common frauds: painting the roofs
of mobile homes with a silver paint that is supposed
to reflect the heat; re-coating driveways with paint
that quickly washes away; coating old electrical wir-
ing with a shiny black paint and claiming that the
wire is new.

Most of the unscrupulous criminals who specialize
in this kind of fraud use intimadation and sometimes
force to collect their fees. The best idea is to refuse to deal with any repairman who comes to your
door uninvited.

There have also been a few scattered instances of
confidence men posing as Social Security represent-
atives to bilk elderly people out of their savings.
The district manager of the Social Security Administration in Tucson advises: If anyone comes to your
door and says he is from the Social Security office,
insist upon seeing his credentials, and if there is
any doubt at all in your mind, telephone his office.